The
COMMON
SENSE
TEACHING
of the
BIBLE

The COMMON SENSE TEACHING of the BIBLE

Hannah Whitall Smith

Fleming H. Revell Company
Old Tappan, New Jersey

This book was originally titled *Every-day Religion.*

Library of Congress Cataloging in Publication Data

Smith, Hannah Whitall, 1832–1911.
  The commonsense teaching of the Bible.

  1. Christian life.   I. Title.
BV4501.S6498   1985   248.4   84–18258
ISBN 0–8007–1416–4

Copyright © 1985 by Fleming H. Revell Company
Published by Fleming H. Revell Company
All rights reserved
Printed in the United States of America

Contents

Introduction

The trouble with Hannah Whitall Smith's books is that they are relevant. They would not have been around for a hundred years, more or less, if they weren't.

But why do I call it "trouble"? Isn't it relevance we are always asking for nowadays?

That depends on two things: relevance of what and to what. In her introduction the author says that her aim has been "not so much to get at the doctrinal truths of our religion, as at the everyday, practical commonsense principles." That answers the first question: relevance *of* what? I found these principles to be as thoroughly practical, as thoroughly commonsense, today as they were when she wrote them.

Next question: relevance *to* what? The word implies close logical relationship with, and importance to, the matter under consideration. If the matter under consideration is comfort, an easy doing of my "own thing," without too much interference or inhibition, then the last thing most of us want is Christian principles that are relevant. They are very likely to stand in the way of our comfort, our convenience, and our own (badly distorted) notions of how to find fulfillment. They may present obstacles to the living of our lives the way we want to live them.

If, on the other hand, the matter under consideration is an honest living out of the life of Christ, no matter what it may cost, then what we want and need is teaching that will show us clearly how Christian principles work in practical terms, in other words, the relevance of the Truth of God to the life of one of His followers in the late twentieth century.

Hannah Whitall Smith is a master of this kind of teaching. The book was first published in 1893, yet no author that I know of speaks more penetratingly and understandably to my own needs than does she. Much contemporary writing and preaching, by aiming at relevance to modern life, revises the truth. Mrs. Smith, by aiming at the Truth, shows how it must revise life.

Practical Christianity is never a matter of religious feeling (much popular teaching today notwithstanding). "The divine order is always first to get your facts," she writes, "then to put faith in those facts; and then, as a natural result, will follow the feelings commensurate with the facts."

My husband and I happened to be in the throes of building a house when this book came into my hands. My mind was full of things like whether to have four-inch tiles or six-inch ones, where to put the electrical outlets and the phone jacks (how can you know until you've placed every stick of furniture in every room?), what color paint we wanted on the soffits. I was trying to bring all of these petty concerns to the Lord and trust Him for help in decisions, and then to go on quietly in what I thought of as the more "important" work committed to me (writing an introduction, composing a talk for a convention, ironing a shirt). The truth, of course, is that there is no more important work than learning to trust God. "The true kingdom of God within us can be set up in the region of our will. It is not a question of splendid talents, nor of great deeds, nor of fervent emotions, nor of wonderful illuminations; it is simply to will what God wills, always and in everything, and without reservation. We have nothing really under control but our own wills ... We are called upon to 'set our faces like a flint' to carry out His will, and must respond with an emphatic 'I will' to every 'Thou shalt' of His."

An illustration from Mrs. Smith's life which was startlingly relevant to mine at the moment had to do with carpets. You can find the story on page 187. The passage in Hebrews (10:34) spoke directly to her in the nineteenth century, and to me in the twentieth, of those Christians who "took joyfully the spoiling of their goods," knowing that they had in heaven a better and more enduring substance. The lesson for me was unmistakable. I must put my faith to work on seemingly trivial matters first. I must learn to lay them all in God's hands and quit stewing. If I refused to do this, I might as well not bother with what I considered my *life's* work, for, as the author points out in another chapter, all things are God's servants. The lessons of faith come to us often in "coarse brown packages," in the ordinary affairs of every day. Faith sees in them God's messengers, and responds in obedience.

Try it. Read the book with prayer, and with a willingness to apply its teaching to the ordinary affairs of your own life. There is release from anxiety and confusion (so I found) in this *Commonsense Teaching of the Bible.* There is also—as always when we trust God and make up our minds to obey Him—real freedom. This is a priceless little handbook of liberation.

ELISABETH ELLIOT
Magnolia, Massachusetts
Summer of 1984

The
COMMON
SENSE
TEACHING
of the
BIBLE

Lesson 1

That Ye May Know

FOUNDATION TEXT:—These things have I written unto you that believe on the name of the Son of God; that ye may know that ye have eternal life, and that ye may believe on the name of the Son of God.—1 JOHN 5:13.

One of the most commonsense principles in everyday life is a clear knowledge of one's earthly position and one's earthly possessions. And nothing is plainer in the Bible than that we were meant to have this knowledge in our religious life as well. Uncertainties are fatal to all true progress and are utterly destructive of comfort or peace. And yet it has somehow become the fashion among Christians to encourage uncertainties in the spiritual life, as being an indication of the truest form of piety. There is a great deal of longing and hoping among Christians, but there is not much knowing. And yet the whole Bible was written for the purpose of making us know. The object of a revelation is to reveal. If nothing has been revealed to us by the Bible beyond longings and hopes, it has failed its purpose. But I fear a large proportion of God's children never get beyond these hopes and longings. "I hope my sins will be forgiven some day"; "I hope I may be favored to reach heaven at last"; "I hope God loves me"; "I hope Christ died for me." These are samples of the style of much Christian testimony in the present day. Indeed, I have even known Christians who could never get further than to say, "I hope that I have a hope." If this word were used in the sense that the Bible always uses it, that is, in the sense of firm expectation, it might be all right; but in the use of it which I have described, there is so great an element of doubt, that it does not amount to a Bible hope at all. We need sometimes to bring our words out into the light of common sense to see what we really do mean by them, and I am afraid in very many cases we should find that the word *hope* would mean, being interpreted, "doubt."

> Now we have received, not the spirit of the world, but the spirit which is of God; that we might know the things that are freely given to us of God (1 Corinthians 2:12).

The Holy Spirit is given to Christians, not to make them have longings and hopes only, but to enable them to "*know* the things that are freely given to us of God." Doubts and uncertainties about spiritual things belong to the spirit of this world, knowledge belongs to the spirit which is of God. As long as we fail to say "I know" in regard to spiritual things, just so long are we allowing the "spirit of this world" to rule instead of the spirit which is of God.

> And many other signs truly did Jesus in the presence of his disciples, which are not written in this book: But these are written that ye might believe that Jesus is the Christ, the Son of God; and that believing ye might have life through his name (John 20:30, 31).
> He that believeth on the Son of God hath the witness in himself; he that believeth not God hath made him a liar; because he believeth not the record that God gave of his Son. And this is the record, that God hath given to us eternal life, and this life is in his Son (1 John 5:10, 11).

The "record" God has given us of His Son has been given for the express purpose of making us know that in His Son we have eternal life. "This is the record," *i.e.,* that God hath given to us eternal life in Christ, and whoever believes in Christ has this life; and of course, ought to know it. If we do not believe this record, and consequently do not know that we have eternal life, we are "making God a liar." These are solemn words, and yet, taking the commonsense view of things, what is a doubt of God's record but the making a liar of God? If I doubt the record of one of my friends, I do in effect make that friend a liar, although I may never dare to use the word. The only way in which we can really honor God is to declare that what He says is always true, and that we know it to be true; and are sure therefore that we have eternal life, because He says so, let the seemings to the contrary be what they may.

In the Bible it is always taken for granted that we know. In his first

Epistle John says, "I have not written unto you because ye know not the truth, but because ye know it, and that no lie is of the truth." He could hardly say the same in these days! "We know that the Son of man is come"; "We know that we are of God"; "We know the things that are freely given us of God"; "I know whom I have believed"; "We know that all things work together for good"; "If I should say I know Him not, I should lie"; "We know that when He shall appear we shall be like Him"; "We know that, if our earthly house of this tabernacle were dissolved, we have a building of God, an house not made with hands, eternal in the heavens." The Bible is full of declarations like these; but how would they sound if we should substitute in them all the word *hope* for the word *know?* Never anywhere in the whole Bible are we given the slightest intimation that God's children were to be anything but perfectly sure of their relationship to Him as children, and of His relationship to them as Father. The flood of doubt and questioning, that so often overwhelms Christian hearts in these days, was apparently never so much as conceived of in Bible times nor by Bible Christians, and consequently it was nowhere definitely provided against. The one uniform foundation upon which were based all commands and all exhortations, was the fact, taken for granted, that of course those to whom the commands and exhortations were addressed, *knew* that they were God's children, and that He was their Father.

> I write unto you, little children, because your sins are forgiven you for his name's sake. I write unto you, fathers, because ye have known him that is from the beginning. I write unto you, young men, because ye have overcome the wicked one. I write unto you, little children, because ye have known the Father. I have written unto you, fathers, because ye have known him that is from the beginning. I have written unto you, young men, because ye are strong, and the word of God abideth in you, and ye have overcome the wicked one (1 John 2:12–14).

Even the little children in Bible times were supposed to know that their sins were forgiven, and that God was their Father. In fact, common sense would tell us that the knowledge of one's position and standing in any relation of life is always the essential foundation of all action in that relation; and how Christians ever came to tolerate (if they do not even sometimes inculcate) such a mist of doubt and uncertainty in regard to the soul's relations with God, is incomprehensible to me.

No service could be rightly performed by any Israelite who was doubtful as to his nationality or his family record.

In the first chapter of Numbers we are told that only those Israelites who could "declare their pedigree" might be numbered among the men of war; and in the second chapter of Ezra no one who could not "find his register" and "reckon his genealogy," was allowed to exercise the office of priest. Any doubts and uncertainties on these points made them "as polluted," and consequently unfit to serve (*see* Numbers 1:2, 17, 18; 2:2; Ezra 2:62, 63). I believe the same thing is also true of Christians now. We can neither be numbered among the Lord's soldiers, nor enter into priestly relations with Him, until we also can "declare our pedigree" as children of God, and "reckon our genealogy" as being born of Him.

There seems something very anomalous in the fact of a man undertaking to call people back to their Father's house, who does not know whether he himself has any right there or not. And yet I fear it is far too common a thing for even clergymen not to know anything certain in regard to their spiritual "pedigree" or "genealogy." I knew a congregation of Quakers where at one time a Friend had been for a year or two "exercising his gift in the ministry." Among the Quakers, "ministers" are not made by colleges or by bishops, but, after a man or woman has "exercised their gift" in the congregation for a sufficient length of time, the spiritually minded in that congregation meet together and decide whether, in their judgment, their friend has really received from the Lord a "gift in the ministry"; and if their decision is favorable, that gift is then acknowledged, and that friend becomes an "acknowledged" or "recommended" minister. The case of the Friend I speak of had been laid before the spiritually minded members of his meeting several times for "acknowledgment," but a favorable decision could never be arrived at, because one man invariably declined to sanction it. The Friend in question finally asked this man the reason for his persistent opposition. After a little hesitation, the man replied it had been a great grief to him that he could not unite in acknowledgment of the Friend's gift. "But," said he, "I have listened to thy preaching very carefully, and I have heard thee very often express a 'humble hope' that at some future time the forgiveness of sins and the gift of eternal life might be thy portion; but I have never heard thee express one single time the knowledge or belief that these blessings had really been bestowed upon thee; and I cannot feel that it is right to encourage any man to preach a gospel to others, about which he himself has so little knowledge." This reply left the Friend without excuse, and he inwardly resolved never again to open his mouth to tell others about eternal life in Christ until he could say with assurance that he knew that that eternal life was his own. Ashamed of the uncertainty, which before he had cherished as a sign of humility, he went to the Word of God to see what was there taught. His faith laid hold of the announcement in 1 John 5:1, "Whosoever believeth that Jesus is the Christ, is born of God," and he said, "I do believe that Jesus is the Christ with all my heart; and God says that if I do this I am born of Him; therefore I know I must be His child"; and he was able from that moment boldly to assert it in the face of every seeming to the contrary.

> But when the fulness of the time was come, God sent forth his Son, made of a woman, made under the law, To redeem them that were under the law, that we might receive the adoption of sons. And because ye are sons, God hath sent forth the Spirit of his Son into your hearts, crying, Abba, Father. Wherefore thou art no more a servant, but a son; and if a son, then an heir of God through Christ (Galatians 4:4–7).

"The adoption of sons"—surely this is an adoption about which there can be no uncertainty! One would think that we for whom Christ died could not question a fact so plainly stated, nor refuse in response to call God our Father! And yet how many do refuse, and think it is presumption to call God their Father, or to take their places boldly as His undoubted sons and heirs.

> Therefore, being justified by faith, we have peace with God through our Lord Jesus Christ: By whom also we have access by faith into this grace wherein we stand, and rejoice in hope of the glory of God (Romans 5:1, 2).
> Having therefore these promises, dearly beloved, let us cleanse ourselves from all filthiness of the flesh and spirit, perfecting holiness in the fear of God (2 Corinthians 7:1).

"Having therefore these promises," and, of course, *knowing* that we have them; "being justified by faith," and, of course, *knowing* that we are, this is the necessary ground of all peace and all purity. Had these passages read differently, had the Apostle begun by saying, "Therefore, feeling very doubtful as to whether we are justified or not," could he have gone on to say so triumphantly, "we have peace with God"? Would he not rather have found it necessary to continue in the same doubtful strain, and to say, "We are very hungry for peace with God, but we do not know whether we have it or not"?

If we were to introduce into the Bible the spirit of uncertainty and doubt that fills the churches today, it would revolutionize the Book!

If you will look at the opening verses of each Epistle, you will see that they are all addressed to people of whom it was taken for granted that they *knew*, without a shadow of doubt, their standing as reconciled and forgiven children of God. I give only two samples.

> To all that be in Rome, beloved of God, called to be saints: Grace to you, and peace, from God our Father, and the Lord Jesus Christ (Romans 1:7).
>
> Paul, called to be an apostle of Jesus Christ through the will of God, and Sosthenes our brother, Unto the church of God which is at Corinth, to them that are sanctified in Christ Jesus, called to be saints, with all that in every place call upon the name of Jesus Christ our Lord, both theirs and ours: Grace be unto you, and peace, from God our Father, and from the Lord Jesus Christ (1 Corinthians 1:1-3).

Imagine the Epistles addressed to doubters, and how different their contents would have been!

Again, notice the present tense of assured possession throughout every Epistle. Take, for instance, as a sample, the first seven verses of the Epistle to the Ephesians.

Notice *"hath* blessed," *"hath* chosen," *"having* predestinated us unto the adoption of children," *"hath* made us accepted in the beloved," "we *have* redemption." And these are only samples. Every Epistle is full of similar tenses of present possession.

Again notice how invariably all the exhortations to holiness are based upon an assured knowledge of our position as the children of God.

> Beloved, now are we the sons of God, and it doth not yet appear what we shall be: but we know that, when he shall appear, we shall be like him; for we shall see him as he is. And every man that hath this hope in him purifieth himself, even as he is pure (1 John 3:2, 3).

And grieve not the holy Spirit of God, whereby ye are sealed unto the day of redemption. Let all bitterness, and wrath, and anger, and clamour, and evil speaking, be put away from you, with all malice: And be ye kind one to another, tenderhearted, forgiving one another, even as God for Christ's sake hath forgiven you (Ephesians 4:30–32).

We are not called upon to forgive one another in order to induce Christ to forgive us, but we are to forgive others, because we first know that He has already forgiven us. We are not commanded to be followers of God in order to become His children, but because we know we are His children.

A man cannot act like a king unless he knows that he is a king; and similarly we cannot act like the sons of God unless we know that we are His sons. In fact, the knowledge of our position and standing is the essential foundation of everything else in the Christian life.

The vital question, then, is how we can come to know. Our foundation text tells us, "These things are written that we may know." We must believe the things that are written in the "record" God has given us of His Son. Then we will know. For believing is the same as knowing, where the person we believe is absolutely trustworthy. There are human beings whose word is so absolutely trustworthy, that we would believe them even almost against the testimony of our own senses; and surely God's word can be no less trustworthy.

"God is not a man that he should lie, neither the son of man that he should repent: hath he said, and shall he not do it? or hath he spoken, and shall he not make it good?" (Numbers 23:19.) If I see therefore that He has unmistakably said anything, I may boldly say I know it, even though every feeling I have should declare the contrary.

He that cometh from above is above all: he that is of the earth is earthly, and speaketh of the earth: he that cometh from heaven is above all. And what he hath seen and heard, that he testifieth; and no man receiveth his testimony. He that hath received his testimony hath set to his seal that God is true (John 3:31–33).

Contrast the expression used here, "hath set to his seal that God is true," with the expression we noticed a little while ago, "hath made God a liar." Which is it you do, dear reader?

We often hear the expression used, "I know such and such a thing is true because such or such a person says so," and this, even when we may have no other testimony than that person's word, and in spite of the fact that we are well aware men often lie. But we seem afraid to say, "I know such and such things are true because God says so," although we are perfectly sure it is impossible for Him to lie.

I believe the explanation of this strange inconsistency may be found in the fact that most people do not accept God's testimony as being really final, but look for some feeling or emotion of their own to witness to its truth. "I could believe such and such things to be true, if I could only feel that they were." In earthly matters we never are so foolish as to make facts depend upon our feelings; but in religious matters a great many seem to think this is the right way. How we ever came to think so, I cannot imagine; for a little exercise of common sense would tell us that facts can never in any region depend upon feelings, but feelings must always in all things depend upon facts. The divine order is always first to get your facts; then to put faith in those facts; and then, as a natural result, will follow the feelings commensurate with the facts. This order is always followed in earthly things by every sane person. But curiously enough in religious matters a great many people, otherwise very sensible, reverse this order, and put feelings first, then faith in those feelings, and come to the facts last, looking upon these facts, one would suppose, as the result of their feelings.

To show how foolish this course is, let us imagine a man intending to take a voyage to a distant country, who should go to the docks and get on board the first vessel that came to hand, and should then retire to his stateroom, and sit down with his eyes shut, to try and "feel" whether he was on the right vessel or not! Such foolishness is inconceivable in any sane human being about earthly things, and yet, strange to say, it is looked upon as being all right in regard to heavenly things.

If we receive the witness of men, the witness of God is greater: for this is the witness of God which he hath testified of his Son. He that believeth on the Son of God hath the witness in himself: he that believeth not God hath made him a liar; because he believeth not the record that God gave of his Son. And this is the record, that God hath given to us eternal life, and this life is in his Son. He that hath the Son hath life;

and he that hath not the Son of God hath not life. These things have I written unto you that believe on the name of the Son of God; that ye may know that ye have eternal life, and that ye may believe on the name of the Son of God . . . (1 John 5:9–13).

In the case of going aboard the vessel the "witness of men," or, in other words, the assurance from someone who knew, would be the only source of peace. And in the case of the Christian the "witness of God," or in other words, God's assurance that He hath given to us eternal life in His Son, cannot fail to bring perfect peace, if only we will believe it.

A great many, however, will say, "Ah, yes, I could easily believe it, if only I had the witness in myself, as the Bible says I am to have." *When* are you to have that witness in yourself? before you believe, or after? Does it say, "he that hath the witness in himself shall believe," or does it say, "he that believeth hath the witness"? It makes all the difference which way you read it, whether you put the believing first, or the witness first. The Bible puts the believing first; which do you?

At that day ye shall know that I am in my Father, and ye in me, and I in you (John 14:20).

The day of knowledge will dawn for us when we come to the point of implicitly believing God!

It must be understood, however, that this knowledge will come to us not as a feeling but as a perception. I mean that we shall know it, even though we may not feel it at all. We do not "feel" that two and two make four, but we know it; and to know is far more valuable and stable a matter than merely to feel. What would we think of a teacher in mathematics who told his pupils they were to "feel" whether or not the multiplication table was correct? One's studies in mathematics must be based on a much more stable foundation than feeling, if they are to stand the test of facts; and one's experience in spiritual things must be the same. We ought to be, and we may be, as sure of God and His love, and of our relations to Him, as we are sure that two and two make four. Feelings may do for Sundays, or for exceptional occasions of special religious experience, but knowledge is the only thing that will avail us in our everyday life.

In all the lessons in this book my object is to help souls to this place of knowledge. I want us to lay aside our conventional preconceived ideas of religion, and get if possible at the heart of the matter, the absolute truth; that is, the truth as it is, not in traditions, nor in creeds, nor in prejudices, but as it is in Jesus. May the blessed Holy Spirit be our Guide and Teacher through all this book!

Lesson 2

Soul Food

FOUNDATION TEXT:—Ho, every one that thirsteth, come ye to the waters, and he that hath no money; come ye, buy and eat; yea, come, buy wine and milk without money and without price. Wherefore do ye spend money for that which is not bread? and your labour for that which satisfieth not? hearken diligently unto me, and eat ye that which is good, and let your soul delight itself in fatness.—Isaiah 55:1, 2.

Good common sense must tell us that our souls need daily food just as much as our bodies. If it is a law in physical life that we must eat to live, it is also equally a law in spiritual life.

"Give us this day our daily bread," is a prayer that includes the soul as well as the body, and unless the religion of Christ contains this necessary food for our weekday lives, as well as for our Sunday lives, it is a grievous failure. But this it does. It is full of principles that fit into human life, as it is in its ordinary commonplace aspects; and the soul that would grow strong must feed itself on these, as well as on the more dainty fare of sermons and services and weekly celebrations.

But it is of vital importance that we choose the right sort of spiritual food upon which to feed. If unwholesome physical food injures the physical health, so also must unwholesome mental food injure the spiritual health. There is such a thing as spiritual indigestion, just as there is physical indigestion. More and more the most skillful physicians are urging the fact that the state of our health is largely dependent upon the food we eat; and gradually mankind is learning that to secure good health for our bodies we must eat only health-giving food. This is equally true on the spiritual plane, although it is

23

not so generally recognized. The laws of spiritual hygiene are as real and as inexorable as the laws of physical hygiene, and it is of vital importance to our soul health that we should realize this.

Does not plain common sense teach us that, when people feed their souls upon a diet of gossip or of frivolities of any kind, they must necessarily suffer from languor of spiritual life, debility of spiritual digestion, failure of vitality, and a creeping moral paralysis?

> And the mixt multitude that was among them fell a lusting: and the children of Israel also wept again, and said, Who shall give us flesh to eat? We remember the fish, which we did eat in Egypt freely; the cucumbers, and the melons, and the leeks, and the onions, and the garlick: But now our soul is dried away: there is nothing at all, beside this manna, before our eyes (Numbers 11:4-6).

> But lusted exceedingly in the wilderness, and tempted God in the desert. And he gave them their request; but sent leanness into their soul (Psalms 106:14, 15).

"Leanness of soul" arises far more often than we think from the indigestible nature of the spiritual food we have been feeding upon. We are not satisfied to eat the food God has provided for us, and we hunger for the fleshpots of Egypt. (*See* also Exodus 16:3, and Numbers 21:5.)

We do not like our providential surroundings perhaps, or our church, or our preacher, or our work, or our family associations, and we are all the time thinking we could be better Christians if only our circumstances were different, if we could attend a different church, or move into a different neighborhood, or engage in a different sort of work. Our souls "loathe the light food" of God's providing; and we question, as the Israelites did, whether God is really able to provide the spiritual food necessary for us in the "wilderness," where He seems to have appointed our dwelling place.

> Yea, they spake against God; they said, Can God furnish a table in the wilderness? Behold, he smote the rock, that the waters gushed out, and the streams overflowed; can he give bread also? can he provide flesh for his people? Therefore the Lord heard this, and was wroth . . . (Psalms 78:19-21).

The "wrath of God" is only another name for the inevitable results of our own bad actions. God's wrath is never, as human wrath generally is, an arbitrary condition of His mind, resulting from His displeasure at being crossed; but it is simply the necessary result of a broken law, the inevitable reaping of that which has been sown. If a man eats unsuitable food he will have indigestion. An untaught savage might say that it was the wrath of God that had brought the indigestion upon him, but we, who understand the laws of health, know that his indigestion is simply the necessary result of the unsuitable food he has eaten. And similarly the sickly spiritual condition of so many Christians is not, as they sometimes think, a direct infliction of God's displeasure, but is simply and only the necessary consequence of the unsuitable and indigestible spiritual food upon which they have been feeding.

> Ephraim feedeth on wind, and followeth after the east wind: he daily increaseth lies and desolation . . . (Hosea 12:1).
> He feedeth on ashes; a deceived heart hath turned him aside, that he cannot deliver his soul, nor say, Is there not a lie in my right hand? (Isaiah 44:20.)

The soul that feeds on the "wind of doctrine," or on the "ashes" of earthly vanity, will find itself brought into a state of great desolation and distress; and this, not because of God's wrath, according to our understanding of that expression, but because of the unchangeable law of spiritual hygiene, that improper soul food must produce illness of soul, just as improper food for the body must make the body ill.

What, then, is the proper food for the soul? What is the daily bread our Lord would have us eat? He tells us in that wonderful discourse in the sixth chapter of John, when He says, "I am the bread of life," and adds, "Whoever eateth me, even he shall live by me." (*See* John 6:48–58.)

To many people this is a very mysterious passage, and I do not at all feel competent to explain it theologically. But it has a common-sense side as well, which has a very practical application to one's everyday life, and it is of this side I want to speak.

Very few persons realize the effect of thought upon the condition of the soul, that it is in fact its food, the substance from which it evolves its strength and health and beauty, or upon which it may become weak and unhealthy and deformed. The things we think about are the things we feed upon. If we think low and corrupt thoughts, we bring diseases upon our soul, just as really as we bring diseases upon our body by eating corrupt and improper food. The man who thinks about self, feeds on self, just in proportion to the amount of thought he gives to self; and may at last become puffed up with self, and suffer from the dreadful disease of self-conceit and self-importance. On the other hand, if we think of Christ we feed on Christ. We eat His flesh and blood practically, by filling our souls with believing thoughts of Him. The Jews said, "How can this man give us His flesh to eat?" And a great many people say the same today. I think my suggestions will show one way at least in which He can give it; and I know that any who try this plan of filling their souls with believing thoughts of Christ will find practically that they do feed upon Him, to the joy and delight of their hearts. He tells us this when He says, "It is the Spirit that quickeneth; the flesh profiteth nothing: the words that I speak unto you, they are spirit, and they are life." He meant them to understand that to feed on Him was to receive and believe His words; that it was not His literal flesh they were to eat, but the words that He spake unto them; that is, the truths that He taught them.

> Thy words were found, and I did eat them; and thy word was unto me the joy and rejoicing of mine heart: for I am called by thy name, O Lord God of hosts (Jeremiah 15:16).
> Moreover he said unto me, Son of man, eat that thou findest; eat this roll, and go speak unto the house of Israel. So I opened my mouth, and he caused me to eat that roll. And he said unto me, Son of man, cause thy belly to eat, and fill thy bowels with this roll that I give thee. Then did I eat it; and it was in my mouth as honey for sweetness (Ezekiel 3:1–3).

If we will take the words of God, that is, His revealed truth, into our lips and eat it; that is, if we will dwell upon His words and say them over and over to ourselves, and thoroughly take in and assimilate their meaning in a commonsense sort of way, we shall find that our soul-life is fed and nourished by them, and is made strong and vigorous in consequence.

> Finally, brethren, whatsoever things are true, whatsoever things are honest, whatsoever things are just, whatsoever things are pure, whatsoever things are lovely, whatsoever things are of good report; if there be

any virtue, and if there be any praise, think on these things (Philippians 4:8).

The things we think on are the things that feed our souls. If we think on pure and lovely things we shall grow pure and lovely like them; and the converse is equally true. Very few people at all realize this, and consequently there is a great deal of carelessness, even with careful people, in regard to their thoughts. They guard their words and actions with the utmost care, but their thoughts, which, after all, are the very spring and root of everything in character and life, they neglect entirely. So long as it is not put into spoken words, it seems of no consequence at all what goes on within the mind. No one hears or knows, and therefore they imagine that the vagrant thoughts that come and go as they list, do no harm. Such persons are very careless as to the food offered to their thoughts, and accept haphazard, without discrimination, anything that comes. Hence, from carelessness about the books they read or the company they keep, they may be continually imbibing as their soul's food the objectionable ideas of the unbeliever, or the sensualist, or the worldly minded, or the agnostic, or the Pharisee. It is not possible to carry this on for any length of time without inducing soul diseases. A vitiation of mind and character is effected, and gradually all delicate distinctions between faith and unfaith, good and evil, purity and impurity, are more and more obliterated. The soul feeds itself on doubt instead of faith, or on coarseness instead of refinement, and becomes correspondingly bewildered or corrupt.

> But those things which proceed out of the mouth come forth from the heart; and they defile the man. For out of the heart proceed evil thoughts, murders, adulteries, fornications, thefts, false witness, blasphemies: These are the things which defile a man; but to eat with unwashen hands defileth not a man (Matthew 15:18–20).
>
> Hear, O earth: behold, I will bring evil upon this people, even the fruit of their thoughts, because they have not hearkened unto my words, nor to my law, but rejected it (Jeremiah 6:19).

The "fruit of our thoughts" is just as sure to come upon us as the fruit of our actions, little as we may have realized it. The laws of hygiene are as absolute in the realm of spirit as in the realm of matter. It is of the utmost importance for us to recognize this, for these laws

work on inexorably, whether we know it or not; and all uncon-
sciously to ourselves we may be at this very moment vitiating and
degrading our soul lives by the thoughts we are indulging, the books
we are reading, or the company we are keeping.

The Apostle sets before us the hope of having all our thoughts
brought into captivity to the obedience of Christ. (*See* 2 Corinthians
10:5.) This cannot mean of course that we are to be thinking of
Christ every minute. A little exercise of common sense will show us
that this is neither possible nor desirable. But it means that we are to
have Christ's thoughts about things instead of our own, that we are
to look at things as He does, and are to judge as He judges. And this
we are to do with "every thought," not with our Sunday thoughts
only, but with our weekday thoughts as well. It would never do for
the health of our bodies to be careful of our food on Sundays only
and pay no regard to what we should eat the rest of the week; and
similarly, it is idiotic to expect our souls to thrive if they are provided
with suitable food on Sundays alone, and are left to feed on ashes
throughout the other days of the week. Neither will little doses of
suitable food now and then do. One hour of a Christlike way of
looking at things will not make much headway in the matter of the
soul's health against ten hours of un-Christlike ways. Every thought
we think, in every hour we live, must be, not necessarily about
Christ, but it must be the thought Christ would think were He placed
in our circumstances and subject to our conditions. This is what it
means really to feed on Him and be nourished by the true bread of
life that cometh down from heaven.

The disciples, when they heard of this living bread, prayed, "Lord,
evermore give us this bread"; and, if we join in their prayer, He can
only reply to us as He did to them, "Here I am; I am the bread of life;
come to me, believe on me, feed your souls with faith in me and with
my thoughts." For again, I would repeat that the most practical way
I know of for feeding on Christ is to fill our souls with His thoughts.
We must do with Him as we would with any great master in art or
science, whose spirit we wished to assimilate, and whose works we
wished to copy. We must study His life, and try to understand His
spirit, and imbue ourselves with His ideas. We must, in short, make
Him our constant mental companion; we must abide with Him and
in Him, and let Him abide in us. We must let the underlying

thoughts of our heart, at the bottom of all other thoughts, be of the Lord and of all His goodness and His love; and all we do and all we think must be founded on these bottom thoughts concerning Him. For again, I repeat, that the things we think about are the things our souls feed upon, and if we want to feed on Christ we must think His thoughts. I do not mean literally have Him consciously in our thoughts every moment, but, rather, as I have said, have faith in Him at the bottom of our thoughts, as the foundation upon which they all rest, and we must accept all His ideas as our own.

> Moreover, brethren, I would not that ye should be ignorant, how that all our fathers were under the cloud, and all passed through the sea; And were all baptized unto Moses in the cloud and in the sea; And did all eat the same spiritual meat; And did all drink the same spiritual drink: for they drank of that spiritual Rock that followed them: and that Rock was Christ (1 Corinthians 10:1–4).

As far as we can gather from their history, the way in which the Israelites in their wanderings ate and drank of Christ, was simply by believing what God said, accepting what He provided, and obeying what He commanded. There was nothing occult or mysterious about it. They did not go off into emotional ecstasies, nor indulge in self-absorbed contemplation. Their spiritual feeding was just a plain matter-of-fact everyday life and walk of trust and obedience. When they ate of the manna they were eating "spiritual meat," for it was the meat God had provided, and the rock from which their water flowed was a "spiritual rock," for it was the rock and the water of God's providing.

This ought to teach us that in the common everyday needs and supplies of life we may as truly feed on Christ as in our moments of spiritual exaltation.

It is in order that some may be helped to eat this same "spiritual meat," and drink this same "spiritual drink," in their everyday lives, that these Bible lessons have been sent out. May the Lord make them His message to each one who shall read them.

What Think Ye of Christ?

FOUNDATION TEXT:—While the Pharisees were gathered together, Jesus asked them, Saying, What think ye of Christ?—Matthew 22:41, 42.

The crucial question for each one of us in our everyday life is just this, "What think ye of Christ?" To some the question may seem to require a doctrinal answer, and I do not at all say that there is no idea of doctrines involved in it. But to my mind the doctrinal answer, valuable as it may be, is not the one of most importance for every day. The vital answer is the one that would contain our own personal knowledge of the character of Christ; not what He is doctrinally, but what He is intrinsically, in Himself. For, after all, our salvation does not depend upon the doctrines concerning Christ, but upon the person of Christ Himself, upon what He is and upon what He does.

> For the which cause I also suffer these things: nevertheless I am not ashamed: for I know whom I have believed, and am persuaded that he is able to keep that which I have committed unto him against that day (2 Timothy 1:12).

Paul knew Him, therefore Paul could trust Him; and if we would trust Him as Paul did, we must know Him as intimately. I am afraid a great many people are so taken up with Christian doctrines and dogmas, and are so convinced that their salvation is secured because their "views" are sound and orthodox, that they have never yet come to a personal acquaintance with Christ Himself; and, while knowing a great deal about Him, it may be, do not know Him Himself at all. They have a sort of religion that will do for church going or for Sunday work, but they have nothing that will do for their weekday living.

For I desired mercy, and not sacrifice; and the knowledge of God
more than burnt offerings (Hosea 6:6).

It is Phillips Brooks, I think, who says, "There are two distinct
ideas of Christianity. One of them magnifies doctrine, and its great
sin is heresy. The other magnifies loyalty, and its great sin is disloy-
alty. The first enthrones a creed. The second enthrones a person."
The first is like a carefully collated botanical manual, the second is
like a living and growing plant. A manual may do for a Sunday religion; nothing but life will do for weekdays. Christ always says, "Believe in me," not, believe this or that about me; but, "Believe in *me*."

Let not your heart be troubled: ye believe in God, believe also in me
(John 14:1).
Jesus saith unto him, I am the way, the truth, and the life: no man
cometh unto the Father, but by me. If ye had known me, ye should
have known my Father also: and from henceforth ye know him, and
have seen him. Philip saith unto him, Lord, shew us the Father, and it
sufficeth us. Jesus saith unto him, Have I been so long time with you,
and yet hast thou not known me, Philip? he that hath seen me hath seen
the Father; and how sayest thou then, Shew us the Father? (John
14:6–9.)

It is not the doctrines concerning Christ, but what He is in Himself, that constitutes the foundation of our faith. "I am the Way, I am
the Truth, I am the Life," He says, "I myself; and if you knew me,
you would know my Father also, and would understand that there
can be nothing in all the universe to make your hearts troubled or
afraid."

Looked at in this light, the question, "What think ye of Christ?"
becomes a question of vital personal import to each one of us. And it
becomes also a question that each one can answer personally and
individually for himself. If it were doctrines only that were in question, we might find it necessary to appeal to the creeds and dogmas of
our own particular sect or denomination in order to find out just
what we do believe, or at least ought to believe. But when it is our
personal estimate of our Lord and Master that is in question, we can
surely each one of us discover very easily what our individual
thoughts about Him are; what is our own opinion of His character
and His ways; what sort of a person, in short, we really think Him to
be. Is He kind and loving, or is He harsh and severe? Is He trustwor-

thy? Is He sympathizing? Is He true to His promises? Is He faithful? Is He self-sacrificing? Is He full of compassion, or is He full of condemnation? Is He our tender brother, or is He our hard taskmaster? Does He care most about Himself, or about us? Is He on our side, or against us?

It is by our answers to questions like these that we shall reveal what our real estimate of Christ is. We may have all the Christian doctrines at our fingers' ends, and yet not have the faintest conception of the real character of Christ Himself. And therefore I would urge upon us a personal answer to this personal question, "What think ye of Christ?"

> Because he hath set his love upon me, therefore will I deliver him: I will set him on high, because he hath known my name (Psalms 91:14).

To "know His name" does not mean to know that He was called Christ or Jesus, but it means to know His character. God's namings always mean character. They are never arbitrary, as our namings are, having no connection with the work or character of the one named. They are always revelations. They tell us what the person is or what he does. "Thou shalt call His name Jesus, for He shall save His people from their sins"; Jesus meaning a Saviour.

> So will I make my holy name known in the midst of my people Israel; and I will not let them pollute my holy name any more: and the heathen shall know that I am the Lord, the Holy One in Israel (Ezekiel 39:7).

To "pollute God's holy name" must mean to attribute to Him a character that is contrary to His goodness. Continually we find the Lord calling upon the people not to profane His name, that is, not to live and act and talk in such a way as to give others a false idea of His character and His works. And continually we find the saints of all ages calling upon the people to "praise His name," which is evidently equivalent to praising Himself. "Both young men and maidens; old men and children; let them praise the name of the Lord; for his name is excellent." "According to Thy name, O God, so is Thy praise unto the ends of the earth." (*See* also Psalms 135:3, 96:8.)

The question, therefore, "What think ye of Christ?" may equally well be rendered by the question, "By what name do you call

Christ?" for name and character are one. What, then, are the names we individually are bestowing upon our Lord? In words, no doubt, and on Sundays we are calling Him our "Lord and Saviour Jesus Christ," but in thought and act in our everyday lives we are unconsciously calling Him by many other names, and some of them, it may be, names that it would shock us very much to hear spoken or to see in print. So few of us, I fear, really know Him!

> Ye call me Master and Lord: and ye say well; for so I am (John 13:13).
> And why call ye me Lord, Lord, and do not the things which I say? (Luke 6:46.)

It is of no use for us to call Him "Master and Lord," while we are refusing to do the things He commands. Our words may hide our thoughts, but our actions reveal them. If we really think He is our Lord, we will not fail to obey Him. It is his thoughts, not his words, that control a man's actions.

> Wherefore the Lord said, Forasmuch as this people draw near me with their mouth, and with their lips do honour me, but have removed their heart far from me, and their fear toward me is taught by the precept of men: Therefore, behold, I will proceed to do a marvellous work among this people, even a marvellous work and a wonder: for the wisdom of their wise men shall perish, and the understanding of their prudent men shall be hid (Isaiah 29:13, 14).

It is very easy to draw nigh to the Lord with our mouths, and honour Him with our lips; but the thoughts of our hearts, what are they? Let us test ourselves by comparing our secret thoughts of Christ with our public words concerning Him. The Bible teaches us to call Him by certain names which express what He is. We reverently and conscientiously, it may be, use these names, as far as words go; but how is it about our thoughts? Do our words express our thoughts, or do our thoughts and our words differ?

Let us take a very familiar instance. The Bible calls Christ by the name of the Good Shepherd, and Christ Himself adopts the name as His own. "I am the Good Shepherd," He says. No doubt, each one of us has called Him by this name hundreds of times. "The Lord is my Shepherd," we have said, over and over and over, times without number, ever since our babyhood. But how about our thoughts? Do they correspond with our words? What do we think of Christ? Do we think of Him as being really and truly our Shepherd, who cares for us as a good shepherd cares for his sheep? Or do we feel as if we ourselves were the shepherds, who must keep a strict watch over Him, in order to make Him faithful to us?

There are certain characteristics that our common sense tells us must be required of every good shepherd. He must devote himself with all his strength and wisdom to the care of his flock. He must forget his own ease and comfort in promoting their well-being. He must protect them from every danger, and must stand between them and all their enemies. He must never forget them nor neglect them, and must be willing to lay down his life for their sakes. Now, is this what we think of Christ when we call Him by the name of Shepherd, if we ever do so call Him, in our everyday life? I very much doubt it! I am afraid we look upon Him in regard to our daily life as an unfaithful shepherd who forgets and neglects his flock; or, as a hireling, who, when he sees the wolf coming, "leaveth the sheep and fleeth"; or as the selfish shepherds of Ezekiel's prophecy, who "fed themselves and fed not the flock." We honor Him on Sundays with our lips, it may be, but alas, the hearts of too many, on weekdays, are far from Him.

> Ye hypocrites, well did Esaias prophesy of you, saying, This people draweth nigh unto me with their mouth, and honoureth me with their lips; but their heart is far from me. But in vain they do worship me, teaching for doctrines the commandments of men (Matthew 15:7–9).

Or again, take the name of Comforter. How many of us take a commonsense view of this name, and really believe that Christ will not and does not leave us comfortless? A comforter must be one who understands our sorrow and our need, and who sympathizes with our sufferings. A comforter must not criticize or judge harshly. He must be tender and considerate, and full of that charity that covers a multitude of faults. A comforter must put arms of love about us, and must whisper in our ears words of infinite kindness. A comforter is for dark times, not for bright times. If anyone should call himself our comforter, and should then run away and hide himself when storms and trials came, we would consider that his name of comforter was merely an empty title, and all his promises of comfort would sound to us like idle tales. What is it that we think of Christ when we read that He has promised not to leave us comfortless, but to come and abide in our hearts as an ever-present Comforter? Do we think of Him as a Comforter for Sundays only, or as One abiding with us through all the week as well? Surely an abiding Comforter must be always with us both on Sundays and weekdays; and if we go uncomforted about anything, it can only be because we do not think He really is our Comforter, however often we may repeat His words about it.

> And I will pray the Father, and he shall give you another Comforter, that he may abide with you for ever; Even the Spirit of truth; whom the world cannot receive, because it seeth him not, neither knoweth him: but ye know him; for he dwelleth with you, and shall be in you. I will not leave you comfortless: I will come to you (John 14:16–18).

Again, take the name of Saviour. If Christ is called by any one name more than another it is Saviour. He is called over and over the Saviour of the world. No one can question that this is, without any controversy, His God-given name. Now, what is the commonsense view of a Saviour? Manifestly, He is One who saves. He is not One who merely offers to save, but He must of necessity, from the very nature of the name, be One who actually does it. The only claim to the name lies in the fact behind the name. We might as rightly call a man a king who had only offered to reign, as to call a man a saviour who has only offered to save. When, then, we say Christ is our Saviour, what are we thinking of Him? Do we think of Him as One who is actually saving us now? Or do we think of Him as One who only offers to save us at some future time, and who has accompanied that offer with such well-nigh impossible conditions that the salvation is practically not available for us at all? Everything in our Christian life depends, not on what we say of Christ, but on what we think of Him when we call Him our Saviour.

> And they that know thy name will put their trust in thee: for thou, Lord, hast not forsaken them that seek thee (Psalms 9:10).
> For our heart shall rejoice in him, because we have trusted in his holy name (Psalms 33:21).
> The name of the Lord is a strong tower: the righteous runneth into it, and is safe (Proverbs 18:10).

The "name of the Lord" can only be a strong tower for us in proportion as we believe that name to express a fact. If I say with my lips that I believe Christ is the Saviour of the world, and at the same time question in my heart whether He saves me, my words are but mere idle tales, and I am really "profaning His holy name." It is an absolute fact that they who "know His name" will, without any doubt, put their trust in Him. No one could help trusting Him as their Saviour, who thought of Him as a real and genuine Saviour who saves.

Had I time I might bring forward many more of the names by which our Lord is called, and press home the same question in connection with each one, "What think ye of Christ?" But enough has been said to show the vital necessity of there being a perfect agreement between our thoughts of Christ and the Bible words concerning Him. Only in this way can we come to know Him. Knowledge is impossible where our thoughts are opposed to the thing we are taught.

> My people are destroyed for lack of knowledge; because thou hast rejected knowledge, I will also reject thee, that thou shalt be no priest to me: seeing thou hast forgotten the law of thy God, I will also forget thy children (Hosea 4:6).
> They shall put you out of the synagogues: yea, the time cometh, that whosoever killeth you will think that he doeth God service. And these things will they do unto you, because they have not known the Father, nor me (John 16:2, 3).

"Because they have not known." Ah, dear friends, how many ugly things we have done, and how many sad things we have suffered, because we have not known Christ! Again I repeat, therefore, that the one absolutely essential thing is to know the Lord. I do not mean know about Him, that avails but little; but to become acquainted with Him Himself, to have a personal knowledge of a personal Saviour, to know what sort of a being He is, to know Him as a man knows his nearest friend, to know Him so intimately as to make it impossible for doubts ever again to assail us.

> And this is life eternal, that they might know thee the only true God, and Jesus Christ, whom thou hast sent (John 17:3).
> Yea, doubtless, and I count all things but loss for the excellency of the knowledge of Christ Jesus my Lord: for whom I have suffered the loss of all things, and do count them but dung, that I may win Christ, And be found in him, not having mine own righteousness, which is of

the law, but that which is through the faith of Christ, the righteousness which is of God by faith: That I may know him, and the power of his resurrection, and the fellowship of his sufferings, being made conformable unto his death (Philippians 3:8–10).

I can well understand how Paul could say so confidently that he counted all things but loss for the excellency of the knowledge of Christ. When once the soul has come to this knowledge, all fear and doubt, and even perplexity, are at an end, and perfect peace must of necessity reign undisturbed.

> Who that one moment has the least descried Him,
>   Faintly and dimly, hidden and afar,
> Doth not despise all excellence beside Him,
>   Pleasures and powers that are not and that are?
> Ay, amid all men, hold himself thereafter
>   Smit with a solemn and a sweet surprise;
> Dumb to their scorn, and turning on their laughter
>   Only the dominance of earnest eyes.

No one can possibly have come to know Christ, as He really is, without entering into absolute rest forever. It is like the rest and peace of the little child in the presence of its mother. The child knows instinctively that its mother will not let anything harm it; therefore it has no fears. And Christians, who know the Lord, know intelligently that He will not let harm come to them; and therefore they can have no fears either. Where there is a perfect caretaker there can be no cares; where there is an invincible protector there can be no anxieties. What is needed then is for Christians to find out that they have just such a Caretaker and Protector in Christ; and this is why Paul could say, and we can all unite with him, that all things are to be counted as loss for the excellency of the knowledge of Christ.

But some may ask, "How can I acquire this knowledge? It seems all so vague and mystical to me that I do not know where to begin." To all such I would reply, that there is nothing mystical about it. Begin by making yourself acquainted with Him in a commonsense way as you would with any historical character you wanted to know. Study His life. Ponder on His words and actions. Find out from the Bible what sort of a person He is, and teach yourself to think of Him as being just what the Bible reveals. And then, counting everything else as loss, accept Him in His fullness as your all-sufficient portion for every day and every hour of your lives.

> For this is the covenant that I will make with the house of Israel after those days, saith the Lord: I will put my laws into their mind, and write them in their hearts: and I will be to them a God, and they shall be to me a people: And they shall not teach every man his neighbour, and every man his brother, saying, Know the Lord: for all shall know me, from the least to the greatest. For I will be merciful to their unrighteousness, and their sins and their iniquities will I remember no more (Hebrews 8:10–12).

It is an essential part of the new covenant that "all should know Him from the least to the greatest." His part is to reveal Himself; our part is to believe His revelations. It is very simple. He tells us He is the Good Shepherd; we are to believe that He actually is, and are to accept Him as our Shepherd. He tells us He is the Saviour who saves now and here, and we are to believe that it is really true, and are to accept His salvation. Of every revelation He has made of Himself in the Bible, we are to say, "This is true; this is true." We are simply to lay aside all our own preconceived ideas, and are to accept God's ideas instead. We are to answer the question, "What think ye of Christ?" by replying, "I think of Him what the Bible tells me to think, and I think absolutely nothing else."

Yield, Trust, Obey

In considering the subject of everyday religion there are three things always absolutely necessary in the attitude of the soul toward the Lord. Other things may be there or may not be there, but these three must. No peace, no victory, no communion are possible where these are absent; and no difficulty is insurmountable where they are present. I often feel like giving out, as a sort of universal commonsense recipe for the cure of all spiritual diseases and difficulties, the three simple words that form the subject of this lesson, *Yield, Trust, Obey.*

YIELD

Now be ye not stiffnecked, as your fathers were, but yield yourselves unto the Lord, and enter into his sanctuary, which he hath sanctified for ever: and serve the Lord your God, that the fierceness of his wrath may turn away from you (2 Chronicles 30:8).

Neither yield ye your members as instruments of unrighteousness unto sin: but yield yourselves unto God, as those that are alive from the dead, and your members as instruments of righteousness unto God (Romans 6:13).

To yield anything means simply to give that thing to the care and keeping of another. To yield ourselves to the Lord, therefore, is to give ourselves to Him, giving Him the entire possession and control of our whole being. It means to abandon ourselves; to take hands off of ourselves. The word *consecration* is often used to express this yielding, but I hardly think it is a good substitute. With many people to consecrate themselves seems to convey the idea of doing something very self-sacrificing, and very good and grand; and it therefore admits of a subtle form of self-glorification. But "yielding" conveys a far more humbling idea; it implies helplessness and weakness, and the glorification of another rather than of ourselves.

To illustrate the difference between the two ideas, let us notice the difference between consecrating one's powers or one's money to some great work, and the yielding of one's self in illness to the care of a skillful physician. In the one case we confer a favor, in the other we receive a favor. In the one case, self can glory; in the other, self is abased. If I were lost in a wild and lonely forest, and a skillful guide should come to my rescue, I could not be said to consecrate myself to that guide, but I would be said to yield myself to his care and guidance. To consecrate is an Old Testament idea, and belongs to the old covenant of works; to yield is a New Testament idea, and belongs to the new covenant of grace. The word, *to consecrate,* is used forty times in the Old Testament, and only twice in the New, and both of these times it refers to Christ. (*See* Hebrews 7:28; 10:20.) The New Testament idea of yielding or surrender is set forth as follows:

> I beseech you therefore, brethren, by the mercies of God, that ye present your bodies a living sacrifice, holy, acceptable unto God, which is your reasonable service (Romans 12:1).

We are to "present" ourselves, to hand ourselves over; to do with ourselves what we do with the money we entrust to the bank, make ourselves over to the care and keeping and use of God. It is not the idea of sacrifice, in the sense we usually give to that word, namely, as of a great cross taken up; but it is the sense of surrender, of abandonment, of giving up the control and keeping and use of ourselves unto the Lord. And this is our "reasonable service," or, as I would express it, our commonsense service. It certainly is the most profound common sense, if we are ill, to put our case into the hands of a skillful physician, or, if we are lost, to put our guidance into the hands of a safe guide; and to put our poor, weak, foolish, helpless selves into the care and keeping of the God who made us, and who loves us, and who alone can care for us, is certainly the most profound common sense of all. To yield to God means to belong to God, and to belong to God means to have all His infinite power and infinite love engaged on our side. A man is bound to take care of anything that belongs to him; and so also, I would say it most reverently, is God. Therefore, when I invite you to yield yourselves to Him, I am inviting you to avail yourselves of an inexpressible and most amazing privilege.

> I speak after the manner of men because of the infirmity of your flesh: for as ye have yielded your members servants to uncleanness and to iniquity unto iniquity; even so now yield your members servants to righteousness unto holiness (Romans 6:19).
> Then Nebuchadnezzar spake, and said, Blessed be the God of Shadrach, Meshach, and Abednego, who hath sent his angel, and delivered his servants that trusted in him, and have changed the king's word, and yielded their bodies, that they might not serve nor worship any god, except their own God (Daniel 3:28).

God always delivers those who, like Shadrach, Meshach, and Abednego, regardless of circumstances or of seemings, yield themselves up into His keeping. Therefore, to yield is our first step.

TRUST

> Commit thy way unto the Lord; trust also in him; and he shall bring it to pass. And he shall bring forth thy righteousness as the light, and thy judgment as the noonday.... And the Lord shall help them, and deliver them: he shall deliver them from the wicked, and save them, because they trust in him (Psalms 37:5, 6, 40).
> Blessed is the man that trusteth in the Lord, and whose hope the Lord is. For he shall be as a tree planted by the waters, and that spreadeth out her roots by the river, and shall not see when heat cometh, but her leaf shall be green; and shall not be careful in the year of drought, neither shall cease from yielding fruit (Jeremiah 17:7, 8).

I might multiply passages concerning trust indefinitely, for the Bible is simply full of them. The word *believe* is often used instead of the word *trust*, but the idea is the same. In the New Testament, especially, the word *believe* is the one generally used; but this does not mean believing in doctrines or believing in history, but, rather, believing in a Person, or, in other words, trusting that Person. Christ always said, "Believe in me," not, "Believe this or that about me," but "Believe in me, in me as a Saviour who can save." You cannot very well trust in "doctrines" or "plans," no matter how much you may believe in them, but you can always trust in the Lord, whether or not you understand His plans or the doctrines concerning Him.

Trusting can hardly be said to be distinct from yielding. It is, in fact, the absolutely necessary correlation to it. It would be impossible for us really to yield ourselves up to the care of a physician or to the guidance of a guide, if we did not trust that physician or that guide; and on the other hand it would be equally impossible for us to trust where we did not yield. Trusting, therefore, simply means that when we have yielded ourselves up unto the Lord, or, in other words, have made ourselves over to Him, we then have perfect confidence that He will manage us and everything concerning us exactly right, and we consequently leave the whole care and managing in His hands. There is nothing but common sense in this. It is what we do a hundred times a day with our fellowmen. We are continually yielding ourselves or our affairs to the care and management of someone else, and feel the utmost unconcern in so doing. We never step into a railway carriage, or aboard a steamer, that we do not take the steps of yielding and trusting. And if we find it an easy and natural thing to do this toward man, how much more easy it must be to do it toward God. Trusting, therefore, is the second step.

OBEY

Know ye not, that to whom ye yield yourselves servants to obey, his servants ye are to whom ye obey; whether of sin unto death, or of obedience unto righteousness (Romans 6:16).

But if thou shalt indeed obey his voice, and do all that I speak: then I will be an enemy unto thine enemies, and an adversary unto thine adversaries. For mine Angel shall go before thee, and bring thee in unto the Amorites, and the Hittites, and the Perizzites, and the Canaanites, and the Hivites, and the Jebusites: and I will cut them off (Exodus 22:22, 23).

Obedience is the logical outcome of yielding and trusting. If I yield myself up into the care of a physician, and trust him to cure me, I must necessarily obey his orders. If I am lost in a wilderness, and surrender myself to the care of a guide, I must walk in the paths he points out. No physician, however skillful, can possibly cure a patient who will not obey his orders; and no guide can lead a lost traveler home, if that traveler refuses to follow his guidance, and persists in walking in paths he forbids. Common sense ought to teach us this. If we want the Lord to care for us, and protect us from our enemies, and provide for our needs, it stands to reason that we must obey His voice, and walk in the paths He marks out for us.

> Oh that my people had hearkened unto me, and Israel had walked in my ways! I should soon have subdued their enemies and turned my hand against their adversaries. The haters of the Lord should have submitted themselves unto him; but their time should have endured for ever. He should have fed them also with the finest of the wheat; and with honey out of the rock should I have satisfied thee (Psalms 81:13–16).

Whatever difficulty we are in, therefore, we must take these three steps. First, we must yield it absolutely to the Lord; second, we must trust Him without anxiety to manage it; and third, we must simply and quietly obey His will in regard to it. A parallel case would be, if one should put a difficult matter into the hands of a lawyer, and should be required by that lawyer to do certain things or to follow certain courses in order to insure the success of the case. Obviously the only commonsense course would be to follow the advice and comply with the suggestions so given, as completely and minutely as possible. To refuse to do so would be to make it impossible for the most skillful lawyer to carry the case to a successful issue. It is of no use, therefore, for us to think of yielding ourselves or any of our affairs to the Lord, and trusting Him to care for us and keep us, unless we make up our minds also to obey Him.

> But this thing commanded I them, saying, Obey my voice, and I will be your God, and ye shall be my people: and walk ye in all the ways that I have commanded you, that it may be well unto you (Jeremiah 7:23).
>
> Behold, I set before you this day a blessing and a curse; A blessing, if ye obey the commandments of the Lord your God, which I command you this day; And a curse if you will not obey the commandments of the Lord your God, but turn aside out of the way which I command you this day, to go after other gods, which ye have not known (Deuteronomy 11:26–28; *see* also Deuteronomy 28:1–14; Jeremiah 38:19, 20).

Obedience, therefore, may be said to be simply a matter of self-interest. It is not a demand made of us, but a privilege offered. Like yielding and trusting, it is simply a way of bringing Divine wisdom and power to bear upon our affairs. And if we could only learn to look upon it in this commonsense kind of way, we should find that it had lost half of its terrors. We should be able to say then with our Divine Master, "I delight to do Thy will," and not merely I consent to do it.

A great many people consent to obey God because they are afraid of the consequences of disobedience, but they find no "delight" in it. If, however, they would only look for a little while on the other side, and see something of the unspeakably blessed consequences of obedience, they would find themselves delighting in obedience, and even embracing it eagerly, and rejoicing in the privilege of it.

> Now, therefore, if ye will obey my voice indeed, and keep my covenant, then ye shall be a peculiar treasure unto me above all people: for all the earth is mine; And ye shall be unto me a kingdom of priests; and an holy nation (Exodus 19:5, 6).

To be "God's peculiar treasure" is surely something to make us delight in obeying His will!

We have now considered the three elements of the little practical, commonsense cure-all, which is the subject of our lesson—Yield, Trust, Obey. It remains for us to learn how to apply the remedy to the disease. All physicians will tell us that a remedy, to be effectual, must be actually and faithfully taken as long as the need continues. In order, therefore, to make this cure-all effectual, we must actually and faithfully take it. That is, we must actually and definitely yield ourselves and all our interests, weekday interests as well as Sunday ones, to God in a continual surrender. We must take our hands off of ourselves, and off of our affairs of every kind, and then we must leave them all in perfect trust to the Lord to manage; and finally we must simply, day-by-day, and hour-by-hour, obey His will as far as we know it. This is to be done about everything, literally everything. We are to keep nothing back. But who could want to keep anything in his own care, when he has the privilege of putting it into God's care?

> Be careful for nothing; but in every thing by prayer and supplication, with thanksgiving let your requests be made known unto God. And the peace of God, which passeth all understanding, shall keep your hearts and minds through Christ Jesus (Philippians 4:6, 7).

This is an infallible recipe. No human being ever acted on it, that peace did not come. No matter how great the trial, no matter how dark the perplexity, no matter even how grievous the sin, if that trial or that perplexity, or that sin, is only yielded up fully to the Lord's management, and He is perfectly trusted to manage it aright, and if the one thus yielding it, quietly and simply obeys God's will in regard to it, as fast as He makes it known, then, just as sure as God is God, will peace and victory come. I except nothing, literally nothing. The Apostle says, "Be careful (*i.e.,* anxious) for nothing." This covers the whole ground: sins, sorrows, perplexities, anxieties, friends, children, property, health, business, Christian work, social life, household cares, plans in life, the past, the future, heights, depths, and "any other creature," all are included, and all must be committed to the care of God. And then, about all, when they are thus committed, the peace of God that passes all understanding will most assuredly come.

Try it, dear readers. About the next thing that troubles you take the three steps I have pointed out. Yield it entirely to the Lord, trust Him about it perfectly, and obey Him implicitly; and persist in this unwaveringly; and then see if, sooner or later, peace and deliverance do not surely come. I have never known it to fail. The deliverance may not always come in your own way, but it will surely come in God's way; and God's way is always the best way, and is the way we ourselves would choose, if we knew all that He knows.

> Cast thy burden upon the Lord, and he shall sustain thee: he shall never suffer the righteous to be moved (Psalms 55:22).
> Casting all your care upon him; for he careth for you (1 Peter 5:7).

Write out the receipt for this universal panacea, and keep it in your pocketbook, and in every moment of need make an application of it. It contains but three words:

YIELD,   TRUST,   OBEY.

All Things Are Thy Servants

FOUNDATION TEXT:—For ever, O Lord, thy word is settled in heaven. Thy faithfulness is unto all generations: thou hast established the earth, and it abideth. They continue this day according to thine ordinances: for all are thy servants.— Psalms 119:89–91.

"All things are thy servants." Not a few things only, but all things. Not things on Sundays only, but things on weekdays as well. We generally think that only the good people or the good things of life can serve God; but here the Psalmist tells us that all things, whether good or bad, are His servants. That is, all things, no matter what their origin may be, are used by the Lord to accomplish His purposes, and all are made to work together for His ends.

And we know that all things work together for good to them that love God, to them who are the called according to his purpose (Romans 8:28).

Both the Psalmist and the Apostle spoke out of the midst of some of the darkest problems and mysteries of life, when they made these declarations. The Psalmist had just been telling how he had been "almost consumed" by the proud, who had "digged pits" for him, and had "persecuted him wrongfully"; and yet in the very face of things, which must have seemed to him so mysterious, he could still declare that God's "faithfulness was unto all generations," and that "all things were His servants."

The Apostle also, out of a deep sense of the "groaning and travailing" of himself and of all creation, under the "bondage of corruption," could declare unhesitatingly his faith, that, not-

46

withstanding these grave mysteries, he still was sure that "all things work together for good to them that love God, to them who are the called according to His purpose."

In both instances it was their profound faith in the God who created and controls the world, that enabled them to see through the blinding mystery, this magnificent fact, that all things are His servants, and that all things must therefore minister to the welfare of His children.

> Praise the Lord from the earth, ye dragons, and all deeps: Fire, and hail; snow, and vapours; stormy wind fulfilling his word (Psalms 148:7, 8).

Even fire and hail, snow and vapor, dragons and all deeps "fulfill His word," and serve Him. And not only is this true of the fierce and cruel things in nature, but of the wicked things in man as well.

> Surely the wrath of man shall praise thee: the remainder of wrath shalt thou restrain (Psalms 76:10).

The "wrath of man" is altogether a wrong thing, and yet even this becomes God's servant, and is forced to accomplish His purposes, and bring Him praise.

> Thou art my battle axe and weapons of war: for with thee will I break in pieces the nations, and with thee will I destroy kingdoms; And with thee will I break in pieces the horse and his rider; and with thee will I break in pieces the chariot and his rider; With thee also will I break in pieces man and woman; and with thee will I break in pieces old and young; and with thee will I break in pieces the young man and the maid; I will also break in pieces with thee the shepherd and his flock; and with thee will I break in pieces the husbandman and his yoke of oxen; and with thee will I break in pieces captains and rulers (Jeremiah 51:20–23).

The common sense of this is simply, that while the Lord does not inaugurate evil in order to accomplish His will, He adopts it to "fulfill His word" using a heathen king as His "battle axe" and His "weapons of war" to accomplish His purposes of discipline and chastening towards His people.

There are many striking instances of this in the Bible. The story of Joseph is one of these. His brethren, in their wrath and envy, sold him into Egypt. Nothing could have seemed on the face of it to be more plainly the result of sin, nor more utterly contrary to the will of God than this; and yet at the end, how clearly we are shown that these wicked brethren, while acting out their own wickedness, were really used by God as His servants to bring about a "great deliverance" and to "save much people alive." (*See* Genesis 45:4–8; 50:19, 20.)

"Ye thought evil against me, but God meant it unto good." This is the secret of all those trials which come to us from the wrath or malice of men. They think evil against us, perhaps, but God means it for good; and we can therefore say with Joseph, of each one, "It was not you" who did it, "but God." Knowing this, it is not strange that the Apostle should assert so triumphantly his deliverance from all fear of what man can do unto him.

> Be content with such things as ye have; for he hath said, I will never leave thee, nor forsake thee. So that we may boldly say, The Lord is my helper, and I will not fear what man shall do unto me (Hebrews 13:5, 6).

The death of our Lord Jesus Christ on the cross was another illustration of this truth. It certainly was "by wicked hands" that He was crucified and slain; and yet these "wicked hands" only accomplished, all unconsciously to themselves, God's "determinate counsel" for the salvation of the world.

> Him, being delivered by the determinate counsel and foreknowledge of God, ye have taken, and by wicked hands have crucified and slain (Acts 2:23).
> Therefore doth my Father love me, because I lay down my life, that I might take it again. No man taketh it from me, but I lay it down of myself. I have power to lay it down, and I have power to take it again. This commandment have I received of my Father (John 10:17, 18).

The multitude who cried, "Crucify Him, crucify Him," thought it was they themselves who were taking His life; but He knew that He laid it down of Himself; and that God was merely using their "wicked hands" as His servants, to accomplish His purposes of love and mercy to mankind. The Jews "thought evil" against Him, but "God meant it unto good."

And so I believe it always is. All things are used by God as His servants, let the agencies that started them be what they may. He does not inaugurate the evil, but when that evil is directed against His children, He makes it His "servant" to carry them a blessing.

That this must necessarily be the case, we can easily see from considering a moment, in the light of common sense, the nature of God's relationship to us. He is our Father. His care of us is more watchful and more tender than the care of any human father could possibly be. All things are in His hands, and He controls each one.

> Yea, all kings shall fall down before him: all nations shall serve him (Psalms 72:11).
> The king's heart is in the hand of the Lord, as the rivers of water: he turneth it whithersoever he will (Proverbs 21:1).
> I am the Lord, and there is none else, there is no God beside me: I girded thee, though thou hast not known me: That they may know from the rising of the sun, and from the west, that there is none beside me. I am the Lord, and there is none else. I form the light, and create darkness: I make peace, and create evil: I the Lord do all these things (Isaiah 45:5–7; *see* also Isaiah 44:24–28; Isaiah 45:12, 13).

From these Scriptures, and many more, had we time to quote them, it is perfectly plain that all things, whether kings, or nations, or light, or darkness, or peace, or evil, or the earth, or the hosts of heaven, or liars, or diviners, or cities, or rivers, or heathen generals, all are under His control, and all must accomplish His will. And this God is *our Father*. Repeat the words over and over again; this God, whom all things must serve, whether they know Him or not, is our Father. Can we conceive of a good father or mother allowing their servants to injure their children? Do we know of any good parents who do not make their servants serve their children? We answer emphatically, No. Then, can we conceive that God, the ideal Father and mother in one, could do what human fathers and mothers would find impossible? No, a thousand times, No! Then our Heavenly Father's servants must as surely serve us, as the servants of our earthly fathers do. And, since all things are God's servants, all things are therefore our servants as well.

> Therefore let no man glory in men. For all things are yours; Whether Paul, or Apollos, or Cephas, or the world, or life, or death, or things present, or things to come; all are yours; And ye are Christ's; and Christ is God's (1 Corinthians 3:21–23).

"All things are yours," not to trouble you and do you harm, but to bless you and do you good. We feel on the earthly plane of things, that it is enough to say of any one that they belong to the family of a rich and generous man, in order to be sure that all things under this man's control are made to minister to their welfare; and how much more must this be the case with us who belong to God. Everything that is His servant must necessarily be our servant as well.

> And the kingdom and dominion, and the greatness of the kingdom under the whole heaven, shall be given to the people of the saints of the most High, whose kindom is an everlasting kingdom, and all dominions shall serve and obey him (Daniel 7:27).

How few, alas! of the children of God have waked up to know their true position as sharing in this universal "kingdom and dominion" of the Son of man! It is our birthright to find all things made our servants, but instead we allow most things to become our masters. A trial comes or a disappointment, and instead of recognizing it as God's servant, sent to bring us some blessing from His hand, we bow down to it as our tyrannical master, and let it crush us into darkness and despair.

How then should God's servants be received?

> And the Lord God of their fathers sent to them by his messengers, rising up betimes, and sending; because he had compassion on his people, and on his dwelling place: But they mocked the messengers of God, and despised his words, and misused his prophets, until the wrath of the Lord arose against his people, till there was no remedy (2 Chronicles 36:15, 16).

Since all things are God's servants, all things must necessarily be His messengers, and therefore every event and dispensation of life has its message for us, let the aspect of the "messenger" be what it may. Many of our choicest gifts from our dearest friends come to us by the hands of very rough-looking messengers, and are wrapped up in coarse brown packages. Do we, because of this, "despise and misuse" the messengers, and refuse to receive and open the packages? My neighbor who treats me unkindly, or my friend who wrongs me, or my enemy who maligns me, each have a message from God for me, as the clergyman who preaches to me, or the Christian friend who gives me a tract. And as I would not "despise or misuse" the one, neither must I the other. We little know, dear friends, of the rich blessings we lose, because we thus despise and misuse the "servants" who bring them. Perhaps the gift of patience, for which you have prayed long and apparently in vain, is held in the hand of that very disagreeable inmate of your household, whose presence has seemed to you such an unkind infliction. Or it may be that the victory over the world, for which your soul has fervently hungered, was shut up in that very disappointment or loss, against which you have rebelled with such bitterness, that it has brought your soul into grievous darkness instead.

> And when the time of the fruit drew near, he sent his servants to the husbandmen, that they might receive the fruits of it. And the husbandmen took his servants, and beat one, and killed another, and stoned another. Again, he sent other servants more than the first; and they did unto them likewise (Matthew 21:34–36).

Often, after times of special blessing, or after a long course of spiritual culture, the Master of our vineyards sends His "servants" to receive for Him the "fruits of it." He has been trying to teach us gentleness and meekness, and when the "time of the fruit" draws near, He sends a "servant" in the shape of a grievous provocation or a cruel misunderstanding, in order that through our reception of these, He may receive the fruits He has sought to cultivate. But how often, alas! we beat one, and stone another, and fail to recognize or receive them as the "servants" who have come to gather the fruits for our Master, whom yet all the time we are professing to be so eager to serve.

In the story of Job we have a very striking illustration of the truth we are considering. All sorts of misfortunes came upon him, originated by all sorts of agencies. His oxen and his asses were stolen by the Sabeans, his sheep and his servants were burned up by lightning, his camels were carried away by the Chaldeans, his sons and his daughters were crushed by the falling in of the house where they were feasting, and finally Job himself was smitten with sore boils from the crown of his head to the sole of his foot. There were very different instrumentalities employed in bringing these misfortunes to pass, and yet all of them—Satan, the Sabeans, the lightning, the Chaldeans, the great wind from the wilderness, and the sore boils that covered Job's body—all were God's "servants" to accomplish His blessed purpose of maturing the "fruits" of meekness, and patience, and submission, and trust, in the heart of Job, and of bringing him into greater nearness and communion with Himself at last. And Job evidently received them as God's "servants," for he took no notice in any case of the "second causes," but referred his trials right back to God. "The Lord gave," he said, "and the Lord hath taken away; blessed be the name of the Lord." And when his wife tempted him to rebel, he called her, as she was in truth, "a foolish woman," and gave her this triumphant answer, "What! shall we receive good at the hand of God, and shall we not receive evil?"

There are no "second causes" to the children of God. There cannot be, because all the so-called "second causes" are God's "servants," and He could never allow any of them to interfere with His purposes, or frustrate His will. Nothing can touch us without His permission; and, when that permission is granted, it can only be because He, in His love and wisdom, sees that the event He permits contains for us some blessing or some medicine that our souls need; while, if He withholds that permission, then men and devils may rage in vain.

> Whatsoever the Lord pleased, that did he in heaven, and in earth, in the seas, and all deep places (Psalms 135:6).

If God "pleases" to let my trial come, He has in that act adopted my trial as His servant.

One of the greatest difficulties in the Christian life arises from the failure to see this fact. The child of God says, "It would be easy to say 'Thy will be done' to my trials, if I could only see that they come from God. But *my* trials and crosses come almost always from some human hand, and I cannot say 'Thy will be done' to human beings." This is all true; but what if we should see, in every human instrumentality, only one of God's "servants," coming to us with hands full of messages and blessings from Him? Could we not then receive them with submission, and even with thankfulness? The trial itself may be very hard for flesh and blood to bear, and I do not mean that we can be thankful for that, but the blessing it brings is surely always cause for the deepest thankfulness. I may not be able to give thanks for an unkind friend, but I can give thanks for the patience and meekness brought to me through the instrumentality of this friend's unkindness.

> Giving thanks always for all things unto God and the Father, in the name of our Lord Jesus Christ (Ephesians 5:20).
>
> In every thing give thanks; for this is the will of God in Christ Jesus concerning you (1 Thessalonians 5:18).

No one can possibly obey this command to give thanks in everything, who fails to see that "all things are God's servants." But to those who do see this, every event of life, even the most disagreeable, is only a bearer of blessing; and as a consequence, all the days of such are filled with continual thanksgiving.

Perhaps some may ask why it is, if all things are indeed God's servants, sent to bring us some message or some gift, that they themselves never seem to get these gifts or messages. The answer is simply this, that because these gifts and messages have come to them wrapped in coarse and ugly packages, and by the hands of rough-looking messengers, they have refused to receive and open them. Their ears have been so filled with their own complainings, that they could not hear God's message, and their eyes have been so absorbed in looking at the seen suffering and hardness, as to fail to look for the unseen blessing.

It is the truest common sense, therefore, to welcome every event of life as God's servant, bringing us something from Him; and to overlook the disagreeableness of the messenger in the joy of the message, and forget the hurt of the trial in the sweetness of the blessing it brings.

> And lest I should be exalted above measure through the abundance of the revelations, there was given to me a thorn in the flesh, the messenger of Satan to buffet me, lest I should be exalted above measure. For this thing I besought the Lord thrice, that it might depart from me. And he said unto me, My grace is sufficient for thee: for my strength is made perfect in weakness. Most gladly therefore will I rather glory in my infirmities, that the power of Christ may rest upon me. Therefore I take pleasure in infirmities, in reproaches, in necessities, in persecutions, in distresses for Christ's sake: for when I am weak, then am I strong (2 Corinthians 12:7–10).

Paul had learned this lesson, and came at last even to "take pleasure" in the "messenger of Satan" that was sent "to buffet him."

Nothing could possibly have a worse origin than a "messenger of Satan," and nothing certainly would seem at first sight to be more unlikely to be one of God's servants; and yet Paul evidently recog-- nized it as such, and was thankful for it, because he found that, shut up in this very "thorn in the flesh" was the blessed revelation to his soul of the power of Christ resting upon him. For the sake of a simi- lar revelation, who would not welcome a similar thorn!

Receive the next thing that hurts thee then, dear reader, as a "ser- vant" sent from God to bear thee a blessing; and busy thyself, not so much with trying to escape thy sorrow, as with trying to find out the message it brings thee. It may be the sin of man that has originated the sorrow, and of course this sinful action itself cannot be said to be the will of God; but by the time it reaches thee it has become "God's servant" for thee, and holds some gift of love and of blessing. No man or company of men, no angels or devils, no principalities or powers in heaven or on earth, can touch the soul that belongs to God, without first passing through His inspection and receiving the seal of His permission.

For all things are His servants, and His kingdom ruleth over all!

> "Things do go wrong; I know grief, pain and fear;
> I see them lord it sore and wide around."
> From her fair twilight answers Truth, star-crowned,
> "Things wrong are needful where wrong things abound;
> Things go not wrong; but Pain, with dog and spear,
> False faith from human hearts will hunt and hound."
>
> —GEORGE MACDONALD.

Lesson 6

"Me!"

FOUNDATION TEXT:— I communed with mine own heart, saying, Lo, I am come to great estate, and have gotten more wisdom than all they that have been before me in Jerusalem: yea, my heart hath great experience of wisdom and knowledge.—Ecclesiastes 1:16.

There is no subject more vital to an everyday religion than a clear understanding of the right relations of our own individuality to the rest of the world. To most people the greatest person in the universe is themselves. Their whole lives are made up of endless variations on the word ME. What do people think of ME? How will things affect ME? Will this make ME happy? Do people value ME as they ought? Look at MY great estate. Behold MY remarkable experiences. Listen to MY wisdom. Adopt MY views. Follow MY methods. And so on, and so on, through all the varied range of daily life. Always and everywhere this giant ME intrudes itself, demanding attention, and insisting on its rights.

Like Solomon in Ecclesiastes, we "commune with our own hearts" concerning our great possessions of various kinds, our wisdom, our knowledge, our righteousness, our good works; and are profoundly impressed with their great value and importance; and naturally we desire to call the attention of those around us to their magnitude!

The whole book of Ecclesiastes is founded on this devotion to the word ME. In the second chapter, for example, we find the words, *I, me, my, mine* used forty times in seven verses (*see* Ecclesiastes 2:3–11).

The "Preacher," as he calls himself, is trying to solve the problem of earthly happiness. "I sought in my heart," he says, "till I might see what was that good for the sons of men, which they should do under the heaven all the days of their life." And he first of all secures for himself everything that he thinks can in any way conduce to the welfare and happiness of ME; and sums it all up in the seven verses I have mentioned. But at the end, in reviewing it all, he is forced to declare that, "behold, all was vanity and vexation of spirit, and there was no profit under the sun."

A little exercise of common sense would show us that this must be the inevitable result of everything that has ME and ME only for its center. There is never any "profit" in it, but always a grievous loss, and it can never turn out to be anything but "vanity and vexation of spirit." Have we not all discovered something of this in our own experience? You have set your heart, perhaps, on procuring something for the benefit or pleasure of your own great big ME; but when you have secured it, this ungrateful ME has refused to be satisfied, and has turned away from what it has cost you so much to procure, in weariness and disgust. Or you have labored to have the claims of this ME recognized by those around you, and have reared with great pains and effort a high pinnacle, upon which you have seated yourself to be admired by all beholders. And lo! at the critical moment, the pinnacle has tottered over, and your glorious ME has fallen into the dust; and contempt, instead of honor, has become its portion. Never, under any circumstances, has it really in the end paid you to try and exalt your great exacting ME, for always, sooner or later, it has all proved to be "nothing but vanity and vexation of spirit."

Job, as well as Solomon, discovered this. In the twenty-ninth chapter of Job, for instance, we have a passage similar to the one in Ecclesiastes. Here the ME of Job is exalted even above the ME of Solomon. The words *I, me, my, mine,* are used over fifty times, and nothing seems wanting that could conduce to the honor and glory of ME. And yet, in spite of all his self-glorification, Job found at last that those who were younger than himself, and whose fathers he would have disdained to have "set among his dogs," simply "had him in derision." It is always so. Efforts after self-glorification and self-exaltation, always end in bringing the ME so glorified into derision. The onlookers may not say anything, perhaps, and may even seem to acquiesce in the praises self bestows upon its ME; but inwardly they laugh it all to scorn. Have not we ourselves seen people laboring to exalt their ME in the eyes of their friends, by recounting, as Job did, their own successes, and dwelling upon their own gifts and capabilities; and have we not always laughed at them in our secret hearts and been sorry that they could not see themselves as others saw them? May it not be even that we have done something of the same sort ourselves, and that there are many unwritten chapters in our own secret autobiographies that are quite as full of the variations on the personal pronouns I, me, my, as this chapter in the book of Job? Have we ever found, however, that such self-praise was any recommendation, or that our self-exaltation exalted us in the eyes of any one besides ourselves?

In the parable of the Pharisee and the Publican our Lord gives us a picture of the Divine judgment in regard to this exalting of our ME; and declares emphatically, "I tell you ... every one that exalteth himself shall be abased: and he that humbleth himself shall be exalted." (*See* Luke 18:9–14.)

Almost the worst effect of self-praise is that our fancied good grows and swells as we look at it and talk about it; and hence a man, whose eyes and whose thoughts are centered on self, comes to have for the most part a strangely exaggerated notion of the goodness and worthiness of his ME. It is like a sort of spiritual dropsy that swells the soul up to twice its natural size, and which looks, perhaps, on the surface as an increase of health and strength, but is in reality only a symptom of a sore disease. Such a one is suffering from what the French call, *La maladie du moi;* and it is one of the most fatal maladies there is.

> But all their works they do for to be seen of men: they make broad their phylacteries, and enlarge the borders of their garments, And love the uppermost rooms at feasts, and the chief seats in the synagogues, And greetings in the markets, and to be called of men, Rabbi, Rabbi. But be not ye called Rabbi: for one is your Master, even Christ; and all ye are brethren. And call no man your father upon the earth: for one is your Father, which is in heaven. Neither be ye called masters: for one is your Master, even Christ. But he that is greatest among you shall be your servant. And whosoever shall exalt himself shall be abased: and he that shall humble himself shall be exalted (Matthew 23:5–12).

It is an inevitable law that he who exalts himself shall be abased. Not always abased outwardly, so that the man himself knows it, but inevitably abased secretly, in the estimation of those around, who are always unfavorably impressed in exact proportion to the efforts self makes to create a favorable impression. How often have we seen pitiful illustrations of this, when Christian workers are together, and each one is vying with the others in trying to edge in some account of the work "*I* have done," or the sermons "*I* have preached," or the meetings "*I* have held," or the honors that have been showered upon ME; and each one thinking all the others so tiresome and so grievously full of self!

> And he put forth a parable to those which were bidden, when he marked how they chose out the chief rooms; saying unto them, When thou art bidden of any man to a wedding, sit not down in the highest room; lest a more honourable man than thou be bidden of him; And he that bade thee and him come and say to thee, Give this man place; and thou begin with shame to take the lowest room. But when thou art bidden, go and sit down in the lowest room; that when he that bade thee cometh, he may say unto thee, Friend, go up higher: then shalt thou have worship in the presence of them that sit at meat with thee. For whosoever exalteth himself shall be abased; and he that humbleth himself shall be exalted (Luke 14:7–11).

ME is a most exacting personage, requiring the best seats and the highest places for itself, and feeling grievously wounded if its claims are not recognized and its rights considered. Most of the quarrels among Christian workers arise from the clamorings of this gigantic ME. "So and so is exalted above ME;" "MY rights have been trampled upon"; "No one considers ME." How much there is of this sort of thing, expressed or unexpressed, in every heart where ME is king! How few of us understand the true glory of taking our seats in the lowest rooms! And yet, if we are to have real "honour in the presence of them that sit at meat" with us, this is what we must do.

> Let nothing be done through strife or vainglory: but in lowliness of mind let each esteem other better than themselves. Look not every man on his own things, but every man also on the things of others. Let this mind be in you which was also in Christ Jesus: Who, being in the form of God, thought it not robbery to be equal with God: But made himself of no reputation, and took upon him the form of a servant, and was made in the likeness of men: And being found in fashion as a man, he humbled himself, and became obedient unto death, even the death of

the cross. Wherefore, God also hath highly exalted him, and given him a name which is above every name (Philippians 2:3–9).

"Lowliness of mind" is the only true road to honor. He that humbleth himself shall be exalted; and no one else. Our Divine Master has set us the example of this; and if we really want to have the "mind that was in Christ Jesus," we must be willing to be made of no reputation, and must take, not the place of mastery, but the place of service.

> But Jesus called them to him, and saith unto them, Ye know that they which are accounted to rule over the Gentiles exercise lordship over them; and their great ones exercise authority upon them. But so shall it not be among you: but whosoever will be great among you, shall be your minister: And whosoever of you will be the chiefest, shall be servant of all. For even the Son of man came not to be ministered unto, but to minister, and to give his life a ransom for many (Mark 10:42–45).

To be the "servant of all" is not a gratifying position to ME. Much more suitable does it seem to this mighty ME that others should serve it, and that it should "exercise lordship and authority" over them. It is only therefore when this tyrannical ME is cast out of our inner kingdom, that we can understand the blessedness and glory of being the "servant of all," or can realize the greatness that comes by this road.

> Likewise, ye younger, submit yourselves unto the elder. Yea, all of you be subject one to another, and be clothed with humility: for God resisteth the proud, and giveth grace to the humble. Humble yourselves therefore under the mighty hand of God, that he may exalt you in due time (1 Peter 5:5, 6).

It seems very hard for Christians to take on this spirit of subjection one to another. The ME in them rebels mightily at any suggestion of such a thing. And yet in the kingdom of heaven it is the only road to greatness.

Our Lord tells us we do well to beware of people who "love salutations in the marketplaces, and the chief seats in the synagogues, and the uppermost rooms at feasts"; and our own instincts tell us the same. Only lately, in discussing the appointment of different Christians to the presidency of an influential society, there was one name mentioned at which every one in the committee exclaimed, almost in a breath, "Oh, we cannot have her, she is far too full of self!"

> A man's pride shall bring him low: but honour shall uphold the humble in spirit (Proverbs 29:23).
> Take my yoke upon you, and learn of me; for I am meek and lowly in heart: and ye shall find rest unto your souls (Matthew 11:29).

To be "meek and lowly in heart" one must get rid of the ME. Some people think they are humble and lowly in heart when they say bitter and disparaging things about themselves, but I am convinced that the giant ME is often quite as much exalted and puffed up by self-blame as by self-praise. The simple truth is, that we ought not to think or talk about our ME at all. Self is so greedy of notice, that, if it cannot be praised, it would rather be blamed, than not noticed at all. It is content to say all manner of ugly things about itself, if only it can by this means attract attention to itself. If it feels a delicacy about saying, "I am so good," it finds almost as much delight in saying, "I am so bad." This seems strange, but I believe the reason is that self feels as if the very saying, "I am so bad," proves that it is not so very bad after all, since it can be so humble! It is, however, a very different thing to say disparaging things about ourselves from having any-one else say them about us. If we are in the habit of making these self-disparaging remarks, let us think for a moment how we should feel if our friends were to agree with our remarks, and were to repeat them to others as their own opinions. Suppose the next time you should say of yourself, "Oh, I am such a poor good-for-nothing creature," some one of your friends should reply, "Yes, that is exactly what I have always thought about you." How would your ME like that? The truth is our ME always expects the disparaging remarks it makes about itself to be denied; and it often, I fear, even if uncon-sciously, makes them for the express purpose of having them denied, and of having its humility, in making such humble statements con-cerning itself, admired and applauded. What can be more delicious to a delicate self-love than to hear itself applauded for having none! The truly meek and lowly heart does not want to talk about its ME at all, either for good or evil. It wants to forget its very existence. As Fénelon writes, it says to this ME, "I do not know you, and am not interested in you. You are a stranger to me, and I do not care what happens to you nor how you are treated." If people slight you or treat you with contempt or neglect, the meek and lowly heart accepts all as its rightful portion. True humility makes us love to be treated, both by God and man, as we feel our imperfections really deserve; and, instead of resenting such treatment, we welcome it and are thankful for it. I remember being greatly struck by a saying of Madame Guyon's, that she had learned to give thanks for every mortification that befell her, because she had found mortifications so helpful in putting self to death. It is undoubtedly true, as another old saint says, that there is no way of attaining the grace of humility but by the way of humiliations. Humiliations are the medicine that the Great Physician generally administers to cure the spiritual dropsy caused by feeding the soul on continual thoughts of ME.

> And thou shalt remember all the way which the Lord thy God led thee these forty years in the wilderness, to humble thee, and to prove thee, to know what was in thine heart, whether thou wouldest keep his commandments, or no. And he humbled thee, and suffered thee to hunger, and fed thee with manna, which thou knewest not, neither did thy fathers know; that he might make thee know that man doth not live by bread only, but by every word that proceedeth out of the mouth of the Lord doth man live (Deuteronomy 8:2, 3).

Many of us may be at this moment taking the same sort of medicine that the Lord was obliged to give to the children of Israel. We need, perhaps, to be "humbled," as much as they did, that we may not be tempted to say in our hearts, "My power and the might of mine hand hath gotten me this wealth"; and the Lord is therefore obliged to "suffer us to hunger," and to "lead us through great and terrible wildernesses" to "prove us, and do us good." Should this be the experience of any of us, we must look at the blessed cure to be wrought, and take our medicine, no matter how bitter may be its taste, with cheerful and thankful hearts.

The Apostle Paul understood the true common sense of humility. He tells us in Philippians the causes he had for self-glorification, but declares that he "counted all these things but dung," so worthless had he discovererd them to be. He bids good-bye to his own gigantic ME, and cries out in language I would we could all adopt, "I am crucified with Christ: nevertheless I live; yet not I, but Christ liveth in me" (Galatians 2:20).

This "yet not I" is one of those "swords of the Spirit" about which Paul speaks when he describes the Christian's armor, and I know none that is more effectual in our conflict with the unruly giant ME. Not even a giant can resist the disintegrating process of an absolute and persistent ignoring of his existence; and if we will but adopt Paul's language, we cannot fail sooner or later to gain Paul's glorious victories.

The Will in Religion

FOUNDATION TEXT:—For to their power, I bear record, yea, and beyond their power, they were willing of themselves.... For if there be first a willing mind, it is accepted according to that a man hath, and not according to that he hath not.—2 Corinthians 8:3, 12.

Fénelon, in a book called *Spiritual Progress,* gives us a deep insight into the place of the will in religion. He says, "True virtue and pure love reside in the will alone." And again, "The will to love God is the whole of religion." This, it seems to me, is the meaning of our foundation text. "If there be a willing mind" it is accepted of God.

And the Lord spake unto Moses, saying, Speak unto the children of Israel, that they bring me an offering: of every man that giveth it willingly with his heart ye shall take my offering (Exodus 25:1, 2).

In a religion that is to fit into everyday life there must be no dependence upon anything emotional or mysterious. A "state of mind" that will carry one safely through a Sunday service will be of no avail against the assaults of Monday's work. In common ordinary life everything depends on the will, which is, as we all know, the governing power in a man's nature. By the will, I do not mean the wish of the man, nor his feelings, nor his longings, but his choice, his deciding power, the king within him to which all the rest of his nature must yield obedience. I mean, in short, the man himself, the "Ego"—that personality in the depths of his being which he feels to be his real self. A great deal of trouble arises from the fact that so few seem to understand this secret of the will. The common thought is that religion resides, not in the will, but in the emotions, and the emotions are looked upon as the governing power in our nature; and consequently all the attention of the soul is directed towards our "feelings"; and, as these are satisfactory or otherwise, the soul rests or is troubled. But the moment we discover the fact that true religion resides in the will alone, we are raised above the domination of our feelings, and realize that, so long as our will is steadfast toward God, the varying states of our emotions do not in the least affect the reality of the divine life in the soul. It is a great emancipation to make this discovery; and a little common sense applied to religion would soon, I think, reveal it to us all. For we must all know that there is something within us, behind our feelings and behind our wishes, an independent self, that after all decides everything and controls everything. The Bible calls this central self the "heart," and declares that out of it are the "issues of life."

> Keep thy heart with all diligence; for out of it are the issues of life (Proverbs 4:23).
>
> A good man out of the good treasure of his heart bringeth forth that which is good; and an evil man out of the evil treasure of his heart bringeth forth that which is evil: for of the abundance of the heart his mouth speaketh (Luke 6:45).

By whatever name philosophers may call this "heart" out of which are the "issues of life," common sense would teach us that it means nothing more nor less than the will; for certainly to my consciousness the will is the governing force in my nature, and the spring of all my actions. It is out of the secret springs of our will that we bring forth the good or evil treasures of our lives. No one who will take a Concordance, and run their eyes down the long list of passages concerning the "heart," can fail to see that when God speaks of the "heart," He means something far other than that bundle of emotions which we of the present day call our hearts. And even we also often use the word *heart* in a far deeper sense. We speak, for instance, of getting "at the heart" of a matter, and we mean, not the feelings that accompany it, but the central idea that dominates it. And in the same way when God speaks of our "hearts," He means our true central self, that "Ego" within us which dominates our whole being. The word is used in the Bible over one thousand times, and it is made to express every form of thought or action that could be predicated of

this central "Ego." The "heart" is said to understand and to be ignorant, to be wise and to be silly, to exercise good judgment or bad, to
be stupefied, to wax gross, to grow fat, to resist the light, to be discouraged, to fluctuate in doubt, to be of the same mind with another,
to seek knowledge, to work wickedness, to devise wicked imagina-
tions, to be set to do evil, to be set to do good, to be astonished, to
tremble, to be glad; it is said, in short, to do and to be exactly what
the man himself is said to do and to be. In numberless instances
where the word *heart* is used, it would not make sense to translate it
by the affections or the emotions.

> And he hath filled him with the spirit of God, in wisdom, in under-
> standing, and in knowledge, and in all manner of workmanship; And to
> devise curious works, to work in gold, and in silver, and in brass, And
> in the cutting of stones, to set them, and in carving of wood, to make
> any manner of cunning work. And he hath put in his heart that he may
> teach, both he, and Aholiab, the son of Ahisamach, of the tribe of Dan.
> Them hath he filled with wisdom of heart, to work all manner of work,
> of the engraver, and of the cunning workman, and of the embroiderer,
> in blue, and in purple, in scarlet, and in fine linen, and of the weaver,
> even of them that do any work, and of those that devise cunning work.
> Then wrought Bezaleel and Aholiab, and every wise hearted man, in
> whom the Lord put wisdom and understanding to know how to work
> all manner of work for the service of the sanctuary, according to all that
> the Lord had commanded. And Moses called Bezaleel and Aholiab,
> and every wise hearted man, in whose heart the Lord had put wisdom,
> even every one whose heart stirred him up to come unto the work to do
> it (Exodus 35:31–35; 36:1, 2).

No one could for a moment suppose that to be "filled with wisdom
of heart," or to be "wise hearted," meant that only the feelings or the
emotions were acted on by God. The man's true inner self must necessarily be meant here. Similarly is this the case in Solomon's prayer
for wisdom. Solomon did not ask, and God did not grant, that
merely his *feelings* should be made wise.

> In Gibeon the Lord appeared to Solomon in a dream by night: and
> God said, Ask what I shall give thee. . . . Give therefore thy servant an
> understanding heart to judge thy people, that I may discern between
> good and bad: for who is able to judge this thy so great a people? And
> the speech pleased the Lord, that Solomon had asked this thing. And
> God said unto him, Because thou hast asked this thing, and hast not

asked for thyself long life; neither hast asked riches for thyself, nor hast asked the life of thine enemies; but hast asked for thyself understanding to discern judgment; Behold, I have done according to thy words: lo, I have given thee a wise and an understanding heart; so that there was none like thee before thee, neither after thee shall any arise like unto thee (1 Kings 3:5–12).

An "understanding heart to discern judgment" involves something far deeper than our feelings or our emotions, let them be ever so lively. It involves the will. Paul thus describes it in Philippians—

Wherefore, my beloved, as ye have always obeyed, not as in my presence only, but now much more in my absence, work out your own salvation with fear and trembling. For it is God which worketh in you both to will and to do of his good pleasure (Philippians 2:12, 13).

The will is the stronghold of our being. If God is to get complete possession of us He must possess our will. When He says to us, "My son, give Me thy heart," it is equivalent to saying, "Surrender thy will to My control, that I may work in it to will and to do of My good pleasure." It is not the *feelings* of a man that God wants, but his will. "Whose adorning," says the Apostle, "let it be the hidden man of the heart in that which is not corruptible, even the ornament of a meek and quiet spirit, which is in the sight of God of great price" (1 Peter 3:3, 4).

The "hidden man of the heart" is the Bible description of the will. It is the interior self, the controlling personality of our being. And the one vital question in our religious experience is, What is the attitude towards God of this "hidden man of the heart"? The very expression, "man of the heart," seems to me full of meaning. It is not the feelings of the heart, but the "man." Our feelings, in fact, do not belong to this "hidden man," but only to the outer or natural man, and are subject to all the varying changes that affect this "outer man." They are therefore of no importance whatever, except as they affect our personal comfort. They are no test of the real condition of the inner "man of the heart." If then our feelings should rebel or become contrary, let us not be perplexed nor discouraged. Our feelings are not ourselves. And what God desires is not fervent emotions, but a pure intention of the will. The whole of His scrutiny falls upon this "hidden man of the heart," and where He finds this honestly devoted to Himself, He disregards all the clamor of our feelings, and is satisfied.

My son, attend to my words; incline thine ear unto my sayings. Let them not depart from thine eyes; keep them in the midst of thine heart (Proverbs 4:20, 21).

To keep God's words in the "midst of our hearts" means a far more stable and real thing than merely to have our emotions stirred up about them.

It is very possible to pour out our emotions upon a matter without really giving our hearts at all. We sometimes see people who are very lavish of their feelings, but whose wills remain untouched. We call this sentimentality, and we mean that there is no reality in it. To get at reality, the heart, or in other words, the will, must be reached. What the will does is real, and nothing else is.

Then the people rejoiced, for that they offered willingly, because with perfect heart they offered willingly to the Lord: and David the king also rejoiced with great joy (1 Chronicles 29:9).
Every man according as he purposeth in his heart, so let him give; not grudgingly, or of necessity: for God loveth a cheerful giver (2 Corinthians 9:7).

"Of his own voluntary will," "according as he purposeth in his heart," these are interchangeable expressions, meant to teach the incontrovertible truth, that it is only things done by "our own voluntary will" that are done by our real selves at all. That which is done from any mere surface motive is simply an outward performance, that has no real meaning, and that cannot be acceptable to the God who looks only at the heart. The true Kingdom of God within us can only be set up in the region of our will. It is not a question of splendid talents, nor of great deeds, nor of fervent emotions, nor of wonderful illuminations; it is simply to will what God wills, always and in everything, and without reservation. We have nothing really under our own control but our wills. Our feelings are controlled by many other things, by the state of our health, or the state of the weather, or by the influence of other personalities upon us; but our will is our own. All that lies in our power is the direction of our will. The important question is not what we feel, nor what are our experiences, but whether we will whatever God wills. This was the crowning glory of Christ, that His will was set to do the will of His Father.

> Sacrifice and offering thou didst not desire; mine ears hast thou opened: burnt offering and sin offering hast thou not required. Then said I, Lo, I come; in the volume of the book it is written of me, I delight to do thy will, O my God: yea, thy law is within my heart (Psalms 40:6–8).

Fénelon says: "I do not ask from you a love that is tender and emotional, but only that your will should lean towards love. The purest of all loves is a will so filled with the will of God that there remains nothing else." We "delight" to do the will of God, not because our piety is so exalted, but because we have the sense to see that His will is the best; and therefore what He wants we want also. And this sort of delight, while it may not be as pleasing to ourselves, is far more satisfactory to Him than any amount of delight in joyous emotions or gratifying illuminations.

But someone will ask whether we are not told to give up our wills. To this I answer, Yes, but in giving up our wills we are not meant to become empty of willpower, and to be left poor, flabby, nerveless creatures who have no will. We are simply meant to substitute for our own foolish misdirected wills of ignorance and immaturity, the perfect and beautiful and wise will of God. It is not willpower in the abstract we are to give up, but our misguided use of that willpower. The will we are to give up is our will as it is misdirected, and so parted off from God's will, not our will when it is one with God's will. For when our will is in harmony with His will, when it has the stamp of oneness with Him, it would be wrong for us to give it up.

The child is required to give up the misdirected will that belongs to it as an ignorant child, and we cannot let it say "I will" or "I will not"; but when its will is in harmony with ours we want it to say "I will," or "I will not," with all the force of which it is capable.

Our will is a piece of splendid machinery, a sort of "governor," such as they have in steam engines to regulate the working of the steam; and everything depends upon the intelligence that guides its action; whether it is guided by our ignorance or by God's wisdom. As long as our own ignorance is the guide, the whole machinery is sure to go wrong, and it is dangerous for us to say "I will" or "I will not."

But when we have surrendered the working of our wills to God, and are letting Him "work in us to will and to do of His good pleasure," we are then called upon to "set our faces like a flint" to carry out His will, and must respond with an emphatic "I will" to every "Thou shalt" of His.

> Now the God of peace, that brought again from the dead our Lord Jesus, that great shepherd of the sheep, through the blood of the everlasting covenant, Make you perfect in every good work to do his will, working in you that which is wellpleasing in his sight, through Jesus Christ; to whom be glory for ever and ever. Amen (Hebrews 13:20, 21).
>
> I beseech you, therefore, brethren, by the mercies of God, that ye present your bodies a living sacrifice, holy, acceptable unto God, which is your reasonable service. And be not conformed to this world; but be ye transformed by the renewing of your mind, that ye may prove what is that good, and acceptable, and perfect, will of God (Romans 12:1, 2; also Ephesians 6:6).

"Doing the will of God from the heart," this is the only kind of doing His will that is of any value. The soul that has surrendered its central will to God, is the only soul that can do His will "from the heart." It is for this reason that we say that the essence of true virtue consists, not in the state of our emotions, nor in the greatness of our illuminations, nor in the multitude of our good works, but simply and only in the attitude of the will.

The practical bearing of all this upon our religious experience is of vital importance. We are so accustomed to consider the state of our emotions as being the deciding test of our religious life, that we very often neglect to notice the state of our will at all; and we thus leave this stronghold of our nature utterly unguarded, while we attend only to the unimportant outposts. The moment, however, that we recognize the fact that the will is king, our common sense will teach us to disregard the clamor of our emotions, and to claim as real the decision of our will, however contrary it may be to the voice of our emotions.

I will take a familiar case as an illustration. A great trial falls upon a Christian. He knows he ought to say, "Thy will be done," in regard to it, and the purpose of his will is to say it; but his feelings are all in rebellion, and it seems to him, when he tries to say it, as if he were a hypocrite, and would be telling an untruth should he persist. Now the real fact is that all this rebellion, being only in the emotions, is not worth the slightest attention. If in his will the sufferer really chooses the will of God, then he himself really chooses it, and he is no hypocrite when he says, "Thy will be done." The real thing in your experience is not the verdict of your emotions, but the verdict of your will; and you are far more in danger of hypocrisy and untruth in yielding to the assertions of your feelings, than in holding fast to the decisions of your will. If your will then at bottom is on God's side, you are no hypocrite at this moment in claiming your position as belonging altogether to Him, and as being entirely submitted to His control, even though your feelings may all declare the contrary.

A Christian lady of my acquaintance was at one time in her life an apparently hopeless victim of doubts and fears. She knew she ought to trust the Lord, and longed to do it, but she seemed utterly unable. After a long period of suffering from this cause, she finally confided her difficulties to a friend, who, as it mercifully happened, understood this secret concerning the will, and who told her that if in her will she would decide to trust, and, putting all her willpower into trusting, would utterly ignore her feelings, she would sooner or later get the victory over all her doubts. The poor doubter listened in silence for a few minutes, and then, drawing a long breath, said with emphasis, "Yes, I see it. If I choose in my will to trust, I really am trusting, even though all my feelings say the contrary. I do choose to trust now. I WILL trust; I will not be afraid again." As she came to this decision, and thus deliberately put her will on the side of God's will, all the darkness vanished, and her soul was brought out into the glorious light of the gospel; a light which was never dimmed again, until her eyes were opened in the presence of the King.

> And if it seem evil unto you to serve the Lord, choose you this day whom ye will serve; whether the gods which your fathers served that were on the other side of the flood, or the gods of the Amorites, in whose land ye dwell; but as for me and my house, we will serve the Lord (Joshua 24:15).
> And Ruth said, Intreat me not to leave thee, or to return from following after thee: for whither thou goest, I will go; and where thou lodgest, I will lodge: thy people shall be my people, and thy God my God: Where thou diest, will I die, and there will I be buried: the Lord do so to me, and more also, if ought but death part thee and me. When she saw

that she was stedfastly minded to go with her, then she left speaking
unto her (Ruth 1:16–18).

Again, I repeat, the whole question lies in the choice of our will.
The thing we are to do is to "choose," without any regard to the state
of our emotions, what attitude our will shall take towards God. We
must recognize that our emotions are only the servants of our will
(which is the real interior king in our being), and that it is the attitude, not of the servants, but of the master that is important. Is our
choice deliberately made on God's side? Is our will given up to Him?
Does our will decide to believe and obey Him? Are we "steadfastly
minded" to serve Him and follow Him? If this is the case, then, no
matter what our feelings may be, we ourselves are given up to Him,
we ourselves decide to believe, we ourselves decide to obey. For my
will is myself, and what my will chooses, I choose.

Your attitude towards God is as real where only the will acts, as
when every emotion coincides. It does not seem as real to us, but in
God's sight it is as real, and often I think all the more real, because it
is unencumbered with a lot of unmanageable feelings. When, therefore, this wretched feeling of unreality or hypocrisy comes, do not be
troubled by it. It is only in the region of your emotions, and means
nothing, except perhaps that your digestion is out of order, or that
there is an east wind blowing. Simply see to it that your will is in
God's hands; that your true inward personality or "Ego" is aban-
doned to His working; that your choice, your decision, is on His side;
and there leave it. Your surging emotions, like a tossing vessel, which
by degrees yields to the steady pull of the anchor, finding themselves
attached to the mighty power of God by the choice of your will, must
inevitably sooner or later come into captivity, and give in their allegiance to Him. It is a psychological fact, not generally known, that
our will can control our feelings, if only we are "steadfastly minded"
so to do. Have you ever tried it in a case where you have got "turned
around," as we call it, in regard to the direction in which you were
going? Many times, when my feelings have declared unmistakably
that I was going in a direction contrary to the facts, I have changed
those feelings entirely by a steadfast assertion of their opposite. And
similarly I have been able many times to control my rebellious feelings against the will of God by a steadfast assertion of my choice to

accept and submit to His will. Sometimes it has seemed to drain to my lips all the willpower I possessed, to say, "Thy will be done," so contrary has it been to the evidence of my senses or of my emotions. But invariably sooner or later the victory has come. God has taken possession of the will thus surrendered to Him, and has worked in me to will and to do of His good pleasure.

May all my readers speedily learn this practical secret concerning the will!

Lesson 8

Rejoice in the Lord

FOUNDATION TEXT:—Finally, my brethren, rejoice in the
Lord . . . —Philippians 3:1.

The consummation of all Christian experience is to bring the soul
to the place where it has learned how to "rejoice in the Lord,"
and to be satisfied with Him alone. "Finally, my brethren," Paul
says, or, in other words, "The summing up, my brethren, of all I have
to say to you is simply this, rejoice in the Lord." Probably, if we had
written the Epistles, our "finally" would have been something very
different. We would have said, "Finally, my brethren, rejoice in your
faithfulness; or, rejoice in your wonderful experiences; or, rejoice in
your earnest work for the Lord; or, rejoice in your growth in grace."
It would almost certainly have been in something about ourselves
that we would have exhorted one another to rejoice. And yet a little
exercise of common sense would show us that any rejoicing which
has self for its foundation must necessarily end in disappointment,
for sooner or later self always disappoints us, no matter how good or
even how pious a self it may be.

> Thus saith the Lord, Let not the wise man glory in his wisdom, nei-
> ther let the mighty man glory in his might, let not the rich man glory in
> his riches: But let him that glorieth glory in this, that he understandeth
> and knoweth me, that I am the Lord which exercise lovingkindness,
> judgment, and righteousness, in the earth: for in these things I delight,
> saith the Lord (Jeremiah 9:23, 24).

The only thing that can bring unfailing joy to the soul is to understand and know God. This is only plain common sense. Everything
for us depends upon what He is. He has created us, and put us in our

73

present environment, and we are absolutely in His power. If He is good and kind, we shall be well cared for and happy; if He is cruel and wicked, we must necessarily be miserable. Just as the welfare of any possession depends upon the character and temper and knowledge of its owner, so does our welfare depend upon the character and temper and knowledge of God. The child of a drunken father can never find any lasting joy in its poor little possessions, for at any minute the wicked father may destroy them all. A good father would be infinitely more to the child than the most costly possessions. And similarly none of our possessions could be of the slightest worth to us, if we were under the dominion of a cruel and wicked God. Therefore, for us to have any lasting joy, we must come to the place where we understand and know "the Lord which exercises loving-kindness, judgment, and righteousness in the earth."

In everyday life this knowledge is especially necessary, for everyday life as a general thing gives us very little to glory in. In our moments of spiritual exaltation we may sometimes seem to ourselves to have great wisdom, or great strength, or great spiritual riches of one kind or another, in which to glory; but when we come down from the "mount of vision" into the humdrum routine of everyday life, these grand spiritual possessions all seem to disappear, and we are left with nothing of them all to glory in.

God alone is unchangeable; what we call "spiritual blessings" are full of the element of change. The prayer which is answered today may seem to be unanswered tomorrow; the promises, once so gloriously fulfilled, may cease to have any apparent fulfillment; the spiritual blessing, which was at one time such a joy, may be utterly lost; and nothing of all we once trusted to and rested on may be left us, but the hungry and longing memory of it all. But when all else is gone God is still left. Nothing changes Him. He is the same yesterday, today, and forever, and in Him is no variableness, neither shadow of turning. And the soul that finds its joy in Him alone, can suffer no wavering.

> Verily, verily, I say unto you, That ye shall weep and lament, but the world shall rejoice: and ye shall be sorrowful, but your sorrow shall be turned into joy. A woman when she is in travail hath sorrow, because her hour is come: but as soon as she is delivered of the child, she remembereth no more the anguish, for joy that a man is born into the

world. And ye therefore now have sorrow: but I will see you again, and your heart shall rejoice, and your joy no man taketh from you (John 16:20–22).

If we want a "joy that no man can take from us," we must find it in something no man can disturb. No element of joy that is subject to human fluctuations can be in the least depended on. The only lasting joy is to be found in the everlasting God. In God alone, I mean, apart from all else; apart from His gifts, apart from His blessings, apart from all that can by any possibility change or alter. He alone is unchangeable; He is the same good, loving, tender God "yesterday, today, and for ever"; and we can rejoice in Him always, whether we are able to rejoice in His gifts and His promises or not. We rejoice in a baby just because it is, not because of anything it has done or can do for us; and something like this, only infinitely deeper and wider, does it mean to rejoice in God.

Thou wilt shew me the path of life: in thy presence is fulness of joy; at thy right hand there are pleasures for evermore (Psalms 16:11).

"In thy presence is fulness of joy," and fullness of joy is nowhere else. Just as the simple presence of the mother makes the child's joy, so does the simple fact of God's presence with us make our joy. The mother may not make a single promise to the child, nor explain any of her plans or purposes, but *she is,* and that is enough for the child. The child rejoices in the mother; not in her promises, but in herself. And to the child, there is behind all that changes and can change, the one unchangeable joy of the mother's existence. While the mother lives, the child will be cared for; and the child knows this, instinctively, if not intelligently, and rejoices in knowing it. And to the children of God as well, there is behind all that changes and can change, the one unchangeable joy that God is. And while He is, His children will be cared for, and they ought to know it and rejoice in it, as instinctively and far more intelligently than the child of human parents. For what else can God do, being what He is? Neglect, indifference, forgetfulness, ignorance, are all impossible to Him. He knows everything, He cares about everything, He can manage everything, and He loves us! Surely this is enough for a "fulness of joy" beyond the power of words to express; no matter what else may be missed besides.

> Although the fig tree shall not blossom, neither shall fruit be in the vines; the labour of the olive shall fail, and the fields shall yield no meat; the flock shall be cut off from the fold, and there shall be no herd in the stalls: Yet I will rejoice in the Lord, I will joy in the God of my salvation. The Lord God is my strength, and he will make my feet like hinds' feet, and he will make me to walk upon mine high places ... (Habakkuk 3:17–19).

Everything may go! There may seem to be no blossoms nor fruit in our lives, our spiritual fields may seem to yield no meat, and there may be apparently no flocks nor herds in our spiritual stalls; but if we know what it is to rejoice, not in any of these things, but in the Lord alone, we shall find, as the prophet did, that our feet are made "like hinds' feet" for swiftness, and we shall walk in "high places" of spiritual triumph.

> And they of Ephraim shall be like a mighty man, and their heart shall rejoice as through wine: yea, their children shall see it, and be glad; their heart shall rejoice in the Lord (Zechariah 10:7).

To rejoice in the Lord is not a pious fiction, nor is it merely a religious phrase. Neither is it anything mysterious or awe inspiring. It is just good plain commonsense happiness and comfort. It is something people around us can see and be glad about. It smoothes away the frowns, and shuts out the sighs. Long faces and gloomy tones of voice disappear in its presence. It is even full of innocent mirthfulness and lightheartedness. I remember my dear father, who was a saint on earth if ever there was one, but I must confess a very jolly one, teaching me once a great lesson about this. It was during what was considered a very solemn occasion, and something struck his sense of the ludicrous, and he gave a merry lighthearted laugh. A friend present reproved him for laughing on such a "solemn occasion," when he turned to me and said in his dear merry voice, calling me by my pet name, "Han, if people who know their sins are forgiven, and that God loves them and cares for them, cannot laugh, I don't know who can." I believe I have never since had a good laugh at anything, that it has not recalled to my mind my father's genuine happiness in knowing himself to be in the care and keeping of his Father in heaven.

> Then he said unto them, Go your way, eat the fat, and drink the sweet, and send portions unto them for whom nothing is prepared: for

this day is holy unto our Lord: neither be ye sorry; for the joy of the Lord is your strength. So the Levites stilled all the people, saying, Hold your peace, for the day is holy; neither be ye grieved. And all the people went their way to eat, and to drink, and to send portions, and to make great mirth, because they had understood the words that were declared unto them (Nehemiah 8:10–12).

Joy is always a source of strength. When we are happy we feel equal to anything; when we are cast down, everything is a burden. This is true on the earthly plane, and of course it is just as true on the spiritual plane; for the psychological laws that govern the two realms are the same. It seems, however, as if many Christians thought the laws of these two realms were exactly opposite to one another, and that depression and discouragement were greater elements of strength in the spiritual life than joy could ever be. Consequently depression and discouragement are looked upon as very pious and humble frames of mind, and joy is considered to be a sort of spiritual bonbon, only to be partaken of at rare and uncertain intervals. It is no wonder that the lives of such Christians languish and are withered.

> The vine is dried up, and the fig tree languisheth; the pomegranate tree, the palm tree also, and the apple tree, even all the trees of the field are withered: because joy is withered away from the sons of men (Joel 1:12).
>
> Because thou servedst not the Lord thy God with joyfulness, and with gladness of heart, for the abundance of all things; Therefore shalt thou serve thine enemies which the Lord shall send against thee, in hunger, and in thirst, and in nakedness, and in want of all things: and he shall put a yoke of iron upon thy neck, until he have destroyed thee (Deuteronomy 28:47, 48).

Notice the use of the words *because* and *therefore,* in these two passages. "Because," the Lord is not served with joyfulness and gladness, "therefore" there can be no fruit, and service becomes "a yoke of iron" upon our necks. This *because* and *therefore* are inseparably connected in the spiritual life. The *therefore* is not an arbitrary sentence of God, but is the natural and necessary result of the *because*. If we will not rejoice and be glad in heart in the Lord, then we shall inevitably be in hunger, and in thirst, and in nakedness, and in want of all things elsewhere. For our souls are of such a divine origin, that no other joy but joy in God can ever satisfy them. It is like trying to satisfy a man of culture with the joys of a savage. He simply could not enjoy them. They would give him no pleasure, but would, instead, bore him and weary him beyond words; and this is why all the joys of earth so soon pall upon us. They cannot satisfy the soul that was made for God. Solomon discovered this.

> And whatsoever mine eyes desired I kept not from them; I withheld not my heart from any joy, for my heart rejoiced in all my labour; and this was my portion of all my labour. Then I looked on all the works that my hands had wrought, and on the labour that I had laboured to do: and, behold, all was vanity and vexation of spirit, and there was no profit under the sun. Therefore I hated life; because the work that is wrought under the sun is grievous unto me: for all is vanity and vexation of spirit (Ecclesiastes 2:10, 11, 17).

If ever a man had his fill of earthly joys, Solomon had, and yet at the end of it all his verdict was, "Behold, all is vanity and vexation of spirit, and there is no profit under the sun." Thousands of people since have given the same testimony. Faber says—

> God only is the creature's home,
>   Though rough and straight the road;
> Yet nothing else can satisfy
>   The soul that's made for God.

God, who made the soul, made it for this high destiny, and His object, therefore, in all the discipline and training of life, is to bring us to the place where we shall find our joy in Him alone. For this purpose He is obliged often to stain our pleasant pictures, and to thwart and disappoint our brightest anticipations. He *detaches* us from all else that He may *attach* us to Himself; not from an arbitrary will, but because He knows that only so can we be really happy. I do not mean by this that it will be necessary for all one's friends to die, or for all one's money to be lost; but I do mean that the soul shall find itself, either from inward or outward causes, desolate and bereft, and empty of all comfort, except in God. We must come to the end of everything that is not God, in order to find our joy in God alone.

> He will swallow up death in victory; and the Lord God will wipe away tears from off all faces; and the rebuke of his people shall he take

away from off all the earth: for the Lord hath spoken it. And it shall be
said in that day, Lo, this is our God; we have waited for him, and he
will save us: this is the Lord; we have waited for him, we will be glad
and rejoice in his salvation (Isaiah 25:8, 9).

To every soul there must come sooner or later a time when we, too,
can say, "Lo, this is our God; we have waited for Him; we will be
glad and rejoice in His salvation." Through all the experiences of life
this is what we are "waiting" for, and all our training and discipline
is to lead us to this. I say "waiting for," not in the sense of any delay
on God's part, but because of the delay on our own part. God is always seeking to make Himself our "exceeding joy," but until we
have been detached from all earthly joys, and are ready to find our
joy in Him alone, we must still "wait for Him." We think that the
delay is altogether on His part, but the real truth is, that all the waiting that is necessary is for Him to wait for us.

Then will I go unto the altar of God, unto God my exceeding joy;
yea, upon the harp will I praise thee, O God, my God (Psalms 43:4).

To "go" to Him is nothing mysterious. It simply means to turn our
minds to Him, to rest our hearts on Him, and to turn away from all
other resting places. It means that we must not look at, or, in other
words, think about and trouble over our circumstances, or our surroundings, or our perplexities, or our experiences, but must look at
and think about the Lord; and must ask ourselves, not, "How do I
feel about this?" but, "How does the Lord feel?" not, "How shall I
manage it?" but, "How will He manage it?"

Behold, God is my salvation; I will trust and not be afraid: for the
Lord Jehovah is my strength and my song; he also is become my salva-
tion. Therefore with joy shall ye draw water out of the wells of salvation
(Isaiah 12:2, 3).

Until we can truly say "God is my salvation"—meaning God only,
and nobody and nothing else—we shall not be able to draw water
out of the wells of salvation. If anything beside God seems to us to be
our salvation, any "experiences," or "blessings," or "good works," or
even "sound doctrines," we are manifestly not drawing water out of
the wells of God's salvation, but are instead trying in vain to draw it

out of broken cisterns that we ourselves have hewed, and that hold no water (Jeremiah 2:13).

> But let all those that put their trust in thee rejoice: let them ever shout for joy, because thou defendest them: let them also that love thy name be joyful in thee (Psalms 5:11; see also Philippians 3:3; Luke 1:46, 47; Isaiah 29:19; Psalms 104:33, 34).

The Bible is full of these declarations concerning rejoicing in the Lord. I can only quote a few of them, but it will repay Bible students to look them up.

In order, however, fully to understand the subject, we must have a clear comprehension of what spiritual joy and gladness really are. Some people seem to look upon spiritual joy as a thing, a sort of lump or package of joy, stored away in one's heart, to be looked at and rejoiced over. Now, as a fact, joy is not a thing at all. It is only the gladness that comes from the possession of something good, or the knowledge of something pleasant. And the Christian's joy is simply his gladness in knowing Christ, and in his possession of such a God and Saviour. We do not on an earthly plane rejoice in our joy, but in the thing that causes our joy. And on the heavenly plane it is the same. We are not to rejoice in our joy, but we are to "rejoice in the Lord, and joy in the God of our salvation." And this joy no man nor devil can take from us, and no earthly sorrows can touch.

All the spiritual writers of past generations have recognized this joy in God, and all of them have written concerning the stripping process that seems necessary to bring us to it. They have called this process by different names, some calling it "inward desolation," and some the "winter of the soul," and some the "dispensation of darkness," but all meaning one and the same thing; and that thing is the experience of finding all earthly joys stained or taken away, in order to drive the soul to God alone.

One of these writers says that the spiritual life is divided into three stages: the stage of joyful beginnings, the stage of desolation, and the stage of joy in God alone. First, there is the stage of beginnings, when the soul is full of sensible delights, and everything in our religious life seems to prosper. Then, as the soul advances in the divine life, there comes very often the stage of desolation, when the Christian seems to pass through a wilderness, and to suffer, it may be, the loss of all things, both inward and outward. And then, if this period of desolation is faithfully traversed, there comes finally, on the other side of it, the stage of an unaltered and unalterable joy and gladness in God. All has been lost in the desert stage, that all may be found in God further on. The only danger is lest the soul in this desert stage should faint and fail under the stress of desolation, and should turn back to the fleshpots of Egypt for its joy. Our writer says quaintly that this desert is filled with the bodies of "frustrate saints"; and I think we can understand what he means.

> And the ransomed of the Lord shall return, and come to Zion with songs and everlasting joy upon their heads: they shall obtain joy and gladness, and sorrow and sighing shall flee away (Isaiah 35:10).

Every ransomed soul must come sooner or later to this place of "everlasting joy"; and if the only path to it lies through the wilderness, then, so be it, we will welcome the wilderness, and traverse it with a cheerful faith. We must learn to have all our joy in the Lord, and to rejoice in Him when all else in heaven and earth shall seem to fail. We must learn to "rejoice in God," just God alone, simply and only because of what He is in Himself, and not because of what He promises or of what He gives. This is the positive command of the gospel. Do we obey it?

> Rejoice in the Lord alway: and again I say, Rejoice (Philippians 4:4).

Can we answer with the Apostle and the Psalmist that we do joy and rejoice in God?

> And not only so, but we also joy in God through our Lord Jesus Christ, by whom we have now received the atonement (Romans 5:11).

> So, Lord, if thou takest from me all the rest,
> Thyself, with each resumption, drawing nigher,
> It shall but hurt me as the thorn of the briar,
> When I reach to the pale flower in its breast.
> To have Thee, Lord, is to have all Thy best;
> Holding it by its very life divine,
> To let my friend's hand go, and take his heart in mine.

The Meaning of Trouble

FOUNDATION TEXT:—Although affliction cometh not forth of the dust, neither doth trouble spring out of the ground; Yet man is born unto trouble, as the sparks fly upward.—Job 5:6, 7.

Trouble is an essential and inevitable thing in this stage of our existence. We are "born" to it. Our everyday life is full of it. It is part of our universal environment. No one escapes it. Common sense would tell us, therefore, that there must be something bound up in trouble which is necessary for us, something without which we should suffer a grievous loss.

It cannot be, as so many seem to think, because of neglect on God's part that trouble should be so universal, for the Bible plainly teaches that it is a part of our birthright. "Man that is born of woman," we are told, "is of few days and full of trouble"; and the Psalmist, in considering this, declares that he knows God's judgments to be right, and that He had afflicted him in faithfulness.

It is very plain, therefore, that troubles come because of God's faithfulness, and not, as so many seem to think, because of His unfaithfulness. We are taught this in a very striking way in the story of Lazarus. Martha evidently thought their trouble had come because the Lord had failed to be present in the moment of need. "Lord," she cried, "if thou hadst been here my brother had not died." But the Lord's absence had not been a mistake or an oversight. He had planned not to be there; and His absence was for a purpose of mercy.

Now a certain man was sick, named Lazarus, of Bethany, the town of Mary and her sister Martha. (It was that Mary which anointed the Lord

82

with ointment, and wiped his feet with her hair, whose brother Lazarus was sick.) Therefore his sisters sent unto him, saying, Lord, behold, he whom thou lovest is sick. When Jesus heard that, he said, This sickness is not unto death, but for the glory of God, that the Son of God might be glorified thereby. Now Jesus loved Martha, and her sister, and Lazarus. When he had heard therefore that he was sick, he abode two days still in the same place where he was.... Then said Jesus unto them plainly, Lazarus is dead. And I am glad for your sakes that I was not there, to the intent ye may believe; nevertheless let us go unto him (John 11:1-15).

He loved them, therefore He stayed away! It was His faithfulness, not His unfaithfulness, that permitted their sorrow to come upon them without hindrance from Him. And we may be sure that what was true of their sorrow is true of our sorrows also. We say in our ignorance, "If Thou hadst been here, this or that would not have gone wrong"; but if we could see into the heart of the Lord we should hear Him saying in reply, "I am glad for your sakes that I was not there." "I am glad." Love can never be glad of anything that hurts its loved ones, unless there is to come out of the hurt some infinitely greater blessing. Therefore we may be sure, no matter how unlikely it may seem, that hidden in every one of our sorrows there is a blessing which it would be a most grievous loss to us to miss.

> For the Lord will not cast off for ever: But though he cause grief, yet will he have compassion according to the multitude of his mercies. For he doth not afflict willingly, nor grieve the children of men (Lamentations 3:31-33).

The Lord afflicts us, not because He likes to, but because He must, because only so can He bestow upon us the blessings that affliction holds in its gift. We must settle down to this as a fact, and never question it. If there had been any other way of giving us the blessings we need, we may be sure our loving and tender Heavenly Father would have adopted it. He does not "willingly" afflict us. There can be, therefore, no other way!

What, then, are the blessings that sorrow and trial bear in their hands? What is the meaning of the trouble of which the world is so full?

The answer is to be found in this one sentence, "For whom the Lord loveth He chasteneth." The meaning of trouble is love. For trouble is not punishment in our sense of the word; it is chastening. To human thought the word *punishment* has a legal sense, and means retribution or vengeance. But God's idea of punishment is the parental idea of chastening. To chasten means, according to Webster, "to inflict pain upon any one in order to purify from errors or faults." God's chastenings, therefore, are for purifying, not for vengeance. "Whom He loves He chastens," not whom He hates, or whom He is angry with. The meaning of trouble, therefore, is plainly that we may be made "partakers of God's holiness." In other words, it is for "character building"; and character building is to us the most important thing in the whole universe. What happens to me is of no account whatever compared to what I am. Therefore good common sense tells me, if I will only listen to it, that no present ease, or comfort, or absence of trial, is to be weighed for a moment against the building up of character for eternity.

> For our light affliction, which is but for a moment, worketh for us a far more exceeding and eternal weight of glory; While we look not at the things which are seen, but at the things which are not seen: for the things which are seen are temporal; but the things which are not seen are eternal (2 Corinthians 4:17, 18).

Anything that is to do such a wonderful thing for us as to work out a far more exceeding and eternal weight of glory, cannot surely be counted otherwise than as a blessing. And all affliction would be so counted, I am very sure, if we had but eyes to see its outcome. The marble may quiver and shrink from the heavy blows of the mallet, but there can be nothing but joy and rejoicing over the beautiful statue that is wrought out thereby.

But some may ask whether this is true of all affliction? We acknowledge that there are troubles which are evidently meant for blessings; but are there not others that from their very nature must be only and always curses? To this I would answer, that I believe all trouble, no matter of what sort or nature, is meant to purify and sanctify us; and that, moreover, it always does so in a greater or less degree, even though we may, most of us, fail to receive all the full benefit that we might have gained had we been more submissive and humble. The prophet tells us the effect of trouble when he says, "Lord, in trouble have they visited thee; they poured out a prayer when thy chastening was upon them" (Isaiah 26:16). I believe this is true, even in those cases where the trouble is the direct result of our own sins. We see that it was so in the many instances where the children of Israel were plunged into trouble by reason of their sins.

> For all this they sinned still, and believed not for his wondrous works. Therefore their days did he consume in vanity, and their years in trouble. When he slew them, then they sought him: and they returned and enquired early after God. And they remembered that God was their rock, and the high God their redeemer (Psalms 78:32–35).
>
> Nevertheless they were disobedient, and rebelled against thee, and cast thy law behind their backs, and slew thy prophets which testified against them to turn them to thee, and they wrought great provocations. Therefore thou deliveredst them into the hand of their enemies, who vexed them: and in the time of their trouble, when they cried unto thee, thou heardest them from heaven; and according to thy manifold mercies thou gavest them saviours, who saved them out of the hand of their enemies (Nehemiah 9:26, 27).

Nothing could be more evident than this, that most, if not all, of these troubles that befell the children of Israel were the direct and legitimate result of their own sins. They were "disobedient and rebelled against God, and cast His law behind their backs," and "therefore God delivered them into the hand of their enemies." But it is equally evident that this very punishment was meant as a chastening to bring them back to their allegiance to Him, and that it always accomplished its purpose. "When he slew them, then they sought Him." It is the Divine way; and it is the way of love.

> Implacable is love!
>   Foes may be bought or teased
> From their malign intent;
>   But he goes unappeased
> Who is on kindness bent.

Hate punishes for vengeance, but love punishes for reformation. God has no feelings of vengeance to satisfy towards us, that He sends trouble upon us. But He has a heart of implacable love, that cannot be satisfied until it sees us perfect. Let us be thankful then that our God loves us enough to chasten us, and let us learn to kiss the rod with which He smites. "He that spareth his rod hateth his son; but he that loveth him chasteneth him betimes." How thankful we ought to be that our Father in Heaven loves us too much to spare the rod, and that His love is wise enough to chasten us betimes!

In that wonderful story by Bunyan of the Pilgrim's progress heavenward, we are told concerning Christian and Hopeful, that at one time they wandered out of the right path, and became so entangled in a net that they could not escape. "Thus they lay bewailing themselves in the net. At last they espied a shining one coming towards them with a whip of small cords in his hand. . . . Then he said to them, 'Follow me, that I may set you in your way again'; so he led them back to the way which they had left. . . . Then I saw in my dream that he commanded them to lie down; which when they did, he chastised them sore, to teach them the good way wherein they should walk; and as he chastised them he said, 'As many as I love I rebuke and chasten; be zealous, therefore, and repent.' This done, he bids them go their way, and take good heed to the other directions of the shepherds. So they thanked him for all his kindness, and went softly along the right way singing."

> Behold, I have refined thee, but not with silver; I have chosen thee in the furnace of affliction. For mine own sake, even for mine own sake, will I do it: for how should my name be polluted? and I will not give my glory unto another (Isaiah 48:10, 11).
> But who may abide the day of his coming? and who shall stand when he appeareth? for he is like a refiner's fire, and like fullers' soap: And he shall sit as a refiner and purifier of silver: and he shall purify the sons of Levi, and purge them as gold and silver, that they may offer unto the Lord an offering in righteousness (Malachi 3:2, 3).
> And I will bring the third part through the fire, and will refine them as silver is refined, and will try them as gold is tried: they shall call on my name, and I will hear them: I will say, It is my people: and they shall say, The Lord is my God (Zechariah 13:9).

To refine anything does not mean to punish it, but only to purify it; to get rid of all its dross and rubbish, and to bring out its full beauty and worth. It is a blessing, not a curse. And instead of its being something God demands of us, it really is something we ought to demand of God. We have a right to be made as pure as God can make us. This is our claim upon Him. He created us, and we have a right to demand that He should make out of us the best He can, and should do this refining work on the creatures He has called into being. It is His duty to burn up our dross, and bring out our full beauty and worth. Love demands that He should.

George Macdonald speaks some strong words concerning this: "Man has a claim on God, a Divine claim for any pain, want, disappointment, or misery that will help to make him what he ought to be. He has a claim to be punished, and to be spared not one pang that may urge him towards repentance; yea, he has a claim to be compelled to repent; to be hedged in on every side, to have one after another of the strong, sharp-toothed sheep-dogs of the Great Shepherd sent after him, to thwart him in any desire, foil him in any plan, frustrate him of any hope, until he comes to see at length that nothing will ease his pain, nothing make life a thing worth having, but the presence of the living God within him; that nothing is good but the will of God; nothing noble enough for the desire of the heart of man but oneness with the eternal. For this God must make him yield his very being, that He himself may enter in and dwell with him."

Trouble and sorrow, therefore, are not our curse, but one of our most cherished rights. We are like statues, "hewn in the rough," which can only be perfectly shaped by means of the chisel's blows; and these blows are surely the statue's right.

> 'Tis that I am not good—that is enough;
> I pry no farther—that is not the way.
> Here, O my potter, is thy making stuff!
> Set thy wheel going; let it whir and play.
> The chips in me, the stones, the straws, the sand,
> Cast them out with fine separating hand,
> And make a vessel of thy yielding clay.

This, then, is the meaning of trouble. It is to make us good. And we have a right to be made good, for it is God's purpose concerning us. Let us therefore accept our trials as a part of our birthright, and give thanks to the Divine Potter that He has set His wheel whirring, and is casting out, with a "fine, separating hand," all the chips, and stones, and sand that mar the perfect purity of our clay.

How changed would be the aspect of all our trials if we could see them in this light! How easy it would be to say "Thy will be done," if we could once recognize the fact that trouble meant only and always blessing for us! I think the Psalmist understood this when he wrote that wonderful 107th Psalm, in which he tells us of how the Lord chastened Israel, when they rebelled against Him and wandered away from Him, and how this chastening always brought them back to cry unto the Lord; and then breaks out after each such recital with the exultant cry, "Oh that men would praise the Lord for his goodness, and for his wonderful works to the children of men!"

In view of all the blessings that troubles and trials have wrought for many of us, can we not also join with our whole souls in this triumphant cry?

Besides this blessed chastening and refining work of sorrow and trouble, I believe it has often another purpose, and that is to thwart us in a course that our Heavenly Father knows would be disastrous, and to turn us into safer and more successful paths. Disappointments are often direct gateways to prosperity in the very things we have thought they were going to ruin forever. Joseph's story is an illustration of this. He had the promise of a kingdom, but instead he received slavery, and cruel treachery, and imprisonment, and it looked as if all hope of a kingdom was over forever. But these very trials were the gateway into his kingdom, and in no other way could he have reached it. God's thwartings are often our grandest opportunities. We start in a pathway that we think is going to lead us to a desired end, but God in His Providence thwarts us, and then we rashly conclude that all is over, and are in despair. But after a little we find that that very thwarting has been the divine opportunity for the success we desired; or, if not for just that, for a far better thing that we would infinitely rather have. He changes the very thing we thought was our sorrow into our crown of joy.

> To appoint unto them that mourn in Zion, to give unto them beauty for ashes, the oil of joy for mourning, the garment of praise for the spirit of heaviness; that they might be called trees of righteousness, the planting of the Lord, that he might be glorified (Isaiah 61:3).
>
> Thou hast turned for me my mourning into dancing: thou hast put off my sackcloth, and girded me with gladness (Psalms 30:11; also Isaiah 35:6, 7).

Many times in my life in practical affairs I have had my "mourning turned into dancing," because I have found that the trial I mourned was really a gateway into the good things I longed for. And I cannot help suspecting that this is far more often the case than we are inclined to think. I knew a man who had both his feet frozen off, and was thwarted in all his plans by the lameness that ensued. He thought his life was ruined, and mourned with unspeakable anguish. But this very trial opened out for him another career which proved finally to be the thing of all others he would have chosen, and which brought him a success far beyond the wildest dreams of his early aspirations. His greatest trouble became his greatest triumph. Instances of this are innumerable. Every life has some.

> For ye shall go out with joy, and be led forth with peace: the mountains and the hills shall break forth before you into singing, and all the trees of the field shall clap their hands. Instead of the thorn shall come up the fir tree, and instead of the brier shall come up the myrtle tree: and it shall be to the Lord for a name, for an everlasting sign that shall not be cut off (Isaiah 55:12, 13).
> For the Lord shall comfort Zion: he will comfort all her waste places: and he will make her wilderness like Eden, and her desert like the garden of the Lord; joy and gladness shall be found therein, thanksgiving, and the voice of melody (Isaiah 51:3).

Since we have so often experienced our deserts to be turned into the garden of the Lord, and have found fir trees and myrtle trees coming up where we thought there were only thorns and briers, the marvelous thing is that we should ever let ourselves be so utterly cast down and overwhelmed when fresh trouble comes. I think it would be a good exercise of soul for us to write out a little record for our own private use of all the times when this marvelous transformation has happened in our experience. It might make us less ready to despair under our next trial.

But the true secret of endurance lies deeper than this. It is to see God's hand in our trouble, and, losing sight altogether of second causes, to accept it directly from Him. Man may be the instrument to bring about our trouble, or we may even be the instruments ourselves, but back of all is God, who controls everything, and who will not let anything reach us that is not meant for blessing to us, either as refining, or chastening, or as providential thwarting. Why should we allow ourselves to be so needlessly unhappy with thinking that our trouble is one in which God has no part? There cannot be any such trouble. If not a sparrow falls to the ground without our Father, even though a stone from the hand of a cruel boy may cause the fall, then not a trial can come to us without Him, even though some cruel or careless hand may start it on its way. By the time the trial reaches us, it has become God's will for us, and is meant to bless us.

> In all their affliction, he was afflicted, and the angel of his presence saved them: in his love and in his pity he redeemed them; and he bare them, and carried them all the days of old (Isaiah 63:9).
> For he hath not despised nor abhorred the affliction of the afflicted; neither hath he hid his face from him; but when he cried unto him, he heard (Psalms 22:24).

It is the "angel of His presence" in all our afflictions that saves us; and this never fails us. No affliction, let its source be what it may, is "abhorred or despised" by Him, and in none does He hide His face from us. Always He is present, if only we will turn to Him. Perhaps we can tell no human being of our trial. Perhaps if we did tell them they would abhor and despise it. But God knows it, and He does not hide His face from us, nor abhor our affliction. The "angel of His presence" will always save us, if only we will let Him, and He will make all things, even the saddest of troubles, those that arise from our own sins, "work together for our highest good."

> Many are the afflictions of the righteous: but the Lord delivereth him out of them all. He keepeth all his bones: not one of them is broken (Psalms 34:19, 20).

Lesson 10

The Hidden God

FOUNDATION TEXT:—Oh that I knew where I might find him! that I might come even to his seat! I would order my cause before him, and fill my mouth with arguments.... Behold, I go forward, but he is not there; and backward, but I cannot perceive him: On the left hand, where he doth work, but I cannot behold him: He hideth himself on the right hand, that I cannot see him.—JOB 23:3–9.

"Oh, that I knew where I might find Him!" This despairing cry was uttered fifteen centuries before Christ; and one can perhaps understand that in those dark days there might have seemed to be some cause for its utterance. But that it should ever be uttered now, by any soul that possesses the Bible, and has even the slightest faith in Christ, would seem impossible, did we not know, alas! that it is only too often the cry of even Christian hearts. In fact, it is almost one of the greatest difficulties in the lives of many Christians, that God seems so to hide Himself from their longing gaze, and that this hiding seems so often to be in anger or in neglect. This is especially the case in our everyday lives. On Sundays, in church services, or in prayer meetings, we may be helped by our environment to feel the presence of God more consciously; but in the ordinary business and bustle of everyday life, we are apt to lose this consciousness; and then, because we do not feel His presence, we think He cannot be there.

Awake, why sleepest thou, O Lord? arise, cast us not off for ever. Wherefore hidest thou thy face, and forgettest our affliction and our oppression? For our soul is bowed down to the dust: our belly cleaveth unto the earth (Psalms 44:23–25).

91

Will the Lord cast off for ever? and will he be favourable no more? Is his mercy clean gone for ever? doth his promise fail for evermore? Hath God forgotten to be gracious? hath he in anger shut up his tender mercies (Psalms 77:7–9).

The natural heart is continually asking such questions as these. Because we cannot see the hand of God in our affairs, we rush to the conclusion that He has lost sight of them and of us. We look at the "seemings" of things instead of at the underlying facts, and declare that, because God is unseen, He must necessarily be absent. And especially is this the case if we are conscious of having ourselves wandered away from Him and forgotten Him. We judge Him by ourselves, and think that He must have also forgotten and forsaken us. We measure His truth by our falseness, and find it hard to believe He can be faithful when we know ourselves to be so unfaithful. But there is neither common sense in this, nor Divine revelation. As regards common sense, how utterly foolish it is, I might even say idiotic, to make our feelings the test of God's actions; as if He came and went in response to the continual changes in our emotions! Such ideas would turn the Omnipotent, ever-present God, into a mere helpless puppet, pulled by the strings of our varying feelings! But this, of course, is inconceivable; and, as regards Divine revelation, is also equally impossible; for the God revealed to us in the Bible is a God who never, under any conceivable circumstances, leaves us, or forgets us, or neglects our interests. He is shown to us there as a tender Shepherd, who performs with the utmost fidelity all a shepherd's duties; who does not forsake His sheep in the cloudy and dark day, nor desert them when the wolf cometh; but who always draws nearer in every time of need, and goes after each sheep that wanders until He finds it. The hireling fleeth when danger appears, because he is an hireling, but the good Shepherd only sticks closer than ever. It is impossible to imagine a good shepherd forgetting or forsaking his sheep. In fact, it is his duty to stick by them under all circumstances, and to watch over them and care for them every moment. And the God who is thus revealed to us as a "good Shepherd" must necessarily be as faithful to His responsibilities as an earthly shepherd is required to be to his. His care of us may be a hidden care, but it is none the less real, and all things in the daily events of our lives are made to work subservient to His gracious purposes toward us. He may seem to have forgotten us, or neglected us, but it can never be anything but a seeming, for it would be impossible for the God who is revealed to us in the face of Jesus Christ to do such a thing.

> But Zion said, The Lord hath forsaken me, and my Lord hath forgotten me. Can a woman forget her sucking child, that she should not have compassion on the son of her womb? yea, they may forget, yet will I not forget thee. Behold, I have graven thee upon the palms of my hands; thy walls are continually before me (Isaiah 49:14–16).

What an overwhelming answer to the cry of any heart that thinks God has forsaken and forgotten it! "Can a woman forget her sucking child?" Impossible, we say. And yet a woman might even do this incredible thing, but the Lord never. And to prove to us how impossible it would be, He tells us that He has graven us on the "palms of His hands"; a place where, even should He try, He could not help continually seeing us.

And yet in spite of the many emphatic assertions such as this with which the Bible is filled, even Christians sometimes allow themselves to think that God has forgotten or neglected them!

I knew a Christian once who had been plunged into the depths of darkness and despair by the temptation to believe that God had forsaken and forgotten him. A trouble had come upon him in a distant land, through no agency of his own, in a matter which he had especially committed to the care of God, and he did not see how it could have happened unless the Lord had forsaken him. He poured out his anguish and his doubts to a friend, and asked in his despair if there was any help. This friend was one who knew God, and who was therefore as sure of His presence and loving care in the times when He seemed to be hidden from sight as in the times when He made Himself more manifest, and he said to his despairing friend, "Do you believe the Bible, my brother?" "Believe the Bible," replied the sufferer, "why, of course I do, but what has that to do with it?" "Everything," replied his friend, "for the Bible says the Lord never leaves us nor forsakes us, and that He is always present everywhere. Now, do you believe He was present in Australia when this event took place?" "He must have been, I suppose," said the poor sufferer rather reluctantly, as though unwilling to admit the fact. "You say," continued the friend, "that you committed this matter to Him, and you are obliged to admit that He was present in Australia at the time. Now, I ask you, did the Lord attend to the matter you had committed to Him, or did He neglect it?" To this there was no reply. After a solemn pause the friend spoke again, "You say God was present in Australia, and you say you had committed this matter to Him. Now I ask you again, as in His presence, did He attend to it or did He neglect it?" "Oh!" answered the sufferer, with a sudden illumination of faith, "I see it all. God was present there, and He did attend to it, of course, and it must be all right, though I cannot see how. The will of God be done! I can trust Him even about this, and can believe that in spite of all seemings to the contrary, He will make it all work together for good."

> By faith he forsook Egypt, not fearing the wrath of the king: for he endured, as seeing him who is invisible (Hebrews 11:27).

This is the vital point, to see "Him who is invisible." Everything hinges on this; and the difference between a triumphant Christian and a despondent one generally arises from the fact that the former has his eyes opened to discern in all things the hidden God, while the latter is full of doubts as to His presence. But since He has Himself said, "I will never leave thee nor forsake thee," surely every one of us is bound to believe Him, and to assert "boldly," in spite of every seeming to the contrary, our unwavering confidence in the fact of His abiding presence and His unfailing care.

> But now thus saith the Lord that created thee, O Jacob, and he that formed thee, O Israel; Fear not, for I have redeemed thee, I have called thee by thy name; thou art mine. When thou passest through the waters, I will be with thee; and through the rivers, they shall not overflow thee: when thou walkest through the fire, thou shalt not be burned; neither shall the flame kindle upon thee. For I am the Lord thy God, the Holy One of Israel, thy Saviour: I gave Egypt for thy ransom, Ethiopia and Seba for thee (Isaiah 43:1–3).

We may be perfectly sure of this, that the time of our need is the time of His closest and tenderest watchfulness. What would we think of a mother who should run away from her children the moment they got into trouble? And yet this hateful thing, which we would resent in any human mother, some of God's own children do not hesitate to ascribe to Him!

> And I will bring the blind by a way that they knew not; I will lead them in paths that they have not known: I will make darkness light before them, and crooked things straight. These things will I do unto them, and not forsake them (Isaiah 42:16).

Even in our blindness and our ignorance of His presence He is watching over us.

A story I heard once from a friend, who was cognizant of all the circumstances concerning the watchful and overruling care of a hidden caretaker, will illustrate what I mean. A very feeble old lady was obliged to take a long and difficult journey alone. She was burdened with a large amount of troublesome luggage, and was supplied with but little money to make traveling easy. She was too reserved to permit anyone to speak to her about the needs and dangers of the journey, which, however, her friends could not but foresee, and too proud to make it possible for any one to offer help. Her friends were at an utter loss to know what to do, when a noble young man, almost a stranger to her, who had heard the circumstances, solved the difficulty by announcing that matters of business required him to take that identical journey at that identical time. He said nothing to the old lady of the plan he had formed to wait on and care for her, as he knew if he did, her pride would take fright. He simply in secret arranged all his plans to fit in with hers. When it was time to start on the journey he had a cart at the door for his own luggage, and a carriage to convey himself to the train, and then said to the old lady in an offhand sort of way, "Oh, by-the-bye, as we are going by the same train, perhaps you might as well let your luggage go with mine, and you yourself might as well take a seat in my carriage." It all looked so accidental that the old lady never dreamed of any prearrangement, and accepted his offer as naturally as he had made it, and was thus saved a weary walk to the train. He found her a seat near himself in the railway car, and kept on the alert all the time to give her comfort and save her fatigue. When he thought she needed refreshment he had some brought in for himself, and asked her as a kindness to pity his loneliness and share it with him. When changes in trains had to be made, he always said, as if casually, "I might as well see to your luggage when I see to my own." When they stopped at a station overnight he took her to the hotel in the carriage ordered for himself. In short, he cared for her throughout as a tender son would have done, and never left her until he saw her safe at her destination; and yet, never once did she suspect that anything he did was more than accidental, or was not even quite natural in a young man, who was traveling the same way, and, feeling lonely, had taken rather a fancy for her company. In fact, so entirely did he make it all seem like a favor done to himself, that she scarcely thanked him, and not for a moment did she realize that all the comfort and ease of her journey, of which she rather boasted afterward, were entirely owing to his care and attentions.

> Hearken unto me, O house of Jacob, and all the remnant of the house of Israel, which are borne by me from the belly, which are carried from the womb: And even to your old age I am he: and even to hoar hairs will I carry you: I have made, and I will bear; even I will carry, and will deliver you (Isaiah 46:3, 4).
>
> O Lord, thou hast searched me, and known me. Thou knowest my downsitting and mine uprising; thou understandest my thought afar off. Thou compassest my path and my lying down, and art acquainted with all my ways. For there is not a word in my tongue, but, lo, O Lord, thou knowest it altogether. Thou hast beset me behind and before, and laid thine hand upon me (Psalms 139:1-5).

All our lives long God has been caring for us, but how little we have appreciated His care! If the old lady in our story had ever found out what she owed to her young friend, would she not, think you, have been sorely grieved that she had not better appreciated his services, and had failed to thank him as he deserved? And shall not we one day have to feel the same grief toward our hidden God?

> Yet thou in thy manifold mercies, forsookest them not in the wilderness: the pillar of the cloud departed not from them by day, to lead them in the way; neither the pillar of fire by night, to shew them light, and the way wherein they should go (Nehemiah 9:19).
>
> For Israel hath not been forsaken, nor Judah of his God, of the Lord of hosts; though their land was filled with sin against the Holy One of Israel (Jeremiah 51:5).

Even though their land was "filled with sin against the Holy One of Israel," still He did not forsake them. Through all the time of Israel's backsliding, although often unable because of the hardness of their hearts to manifest Himself, yet still He was with them, their hidden Caretaker and Protector. The Book of Esther is a striking exemplification of this. The name Esther means secret or hidden, and the whole Book is a story of the hidden presence of God in the midst of His people, at a time when their backsliding had so blinded their eyes, that they could not see Him. Not once in the whole Book is the name of God mentioned, and yet His overruling care and guidance were never more manifest than in the events here recorded. The children of Israel seemed, as far as appears, to have forgotten God, and to have left Him out of all their thoughts; and to them, no doubt, it must have seemed as if He had likewise forgotten them. But behind all their neglect of Him, and His seeming forgetfulness of them, He held the reins of His providence, and by a series of apparently natural events, and by most unlikely means, using a drunken king, a deceiving woman, a sleepless night, an upstart servant, and a malicious enemy as links in the chain, He brought to pass His will concerning them, and saved them in the time of their need. And just so He does continually now for His people, watching over them the most tenderly at the very moments when He seems the most hidden. And this is the case even when the hiding has been caused by our own unfaithfulness or backsliding. We may forsake Him, but He never forsakes us, no matter how much it may seem as if He had.

It seems to me that it is the greatest infidelity to say of God, when He is hidden from our sight, that He has forsaken us. The simple truth is that He could no more forsake us than a loving mother could forsake her child. I remember once a theologian was arguing the matter out with me, and undertook to assert that there were sins for which even a mother would forsake her child; and I can feel to this day the tempest of mother love and indignation that tore my heart, as I burst into tears, and with difficulty restrained myself from ordering him out of my presence at once! And if I, a poor failing human mother, could feel so, how much more must the Heavenly Father feel, who made the mother-heart in me, and who has declared Himself to be a "God of love!"

> And Jesus came and spake unto them, saying, All power is given unto me in heaven and in earth. Go ye therefore, and teach all nations, baptizing them in the name of the Father, and of the Son, and of the Holy Ghost: Teaching them to observe all things whatsoever I have commanded you: and, lo, I am with you alway, even unto the end of the world. Amen (Matthew 28:18–20).

Have not I commanded thee? Be strong and of a good courage; ·be not afraid, neither be thou dismayed: for the Lord thy God is with thee whithersoever thou goest (Joshua 1:9).

Statements such as these might be multiplied indefinitely, for the Bible is simply full of them. And I do not myself see how any child of God can dare, in the face of them, even so much as to suggest that God has forsaken him. It is simply an impossibility; and the only thing to do is to recognize that it is impossible, and never to admit the idea again.

The story of Joseph gives us a very striking illustration of the hidden workings of God. Nothing could seem more like having been forsaken of God than the long series of misfortunes that befell Joseph, beginning with the cruelty of his brethren, and ending with being forgotten in prison. There was no sign or token in it all of anything but the wickedness and malice of men. And yet, when Joseph was trying in after years to comfort the hearts of his brethren, upon whom remorse had seized, he could say, "Now, therefore, be not grieved nor angry with yourselves that ye sold me hither; for God did send me before you to preserve life." And again, "But as for you, ye thought evil against me; but God meant it unto good, to bring to pass, as it is this day, to save much people alive." The Psalmist also, in recapitulating many years afterward the story of Israel, said concerning these events, "He sent a man before them, even Joseph, who was sold for a servant." It certainly looked to the eye of sense, as if the selling of Joseph into Egypt was man's wickedness only. But the hidden God was at work behind all the wickedness and malice of men, using, as He so often does, the wrath of man to accomplish His purposes. Wicked men were, it is true, the actual agents, but God was the real sender. Moreover, in the very places where Joseph seemed to be the most forsaken, in the house of slavery, and the prison of disgrace, right there, we are told, God was with him and blessed him. (*See* Genesis 39.)

If ever any human being would seem to have been justified in thinking God had forsaken him, surely Joseph would. But from all that appears his faith throughout was steadfast, and no doubting thought seems ever to have entered his heart.

Not so with Jacob. In his times of darkness it is evident that his heart was filled with doubts.

ORDER
GIFT COPIES FOR
LOVED ONES
AT THE SAME PRICE

If you agree with us that THE COMMON SENSE TEACHING OF THE BIBLE is an inspirational book about the Christian faith, you might want to order additional copies for friends and family members. Extra copies are available at the same low price of $8.95 plus postage and handling.

Complete the form below, place it in an envelope and mail it today. Send no money now. We will bill you later.

(Detach here and return this portion)

☐ Yes, please send _____ copies of THE COMMON SENSE TEACHING OF THE BIBLE by Hannah Whitall Smith for $8.95 each plus postage and handling. I may take 30 days to pay and may return my order unless completely satisfied.

XH/R4164

_____
Name

_____
Address

_____
City   State   Zip

Mail to:

Grason

A ministry of the Billy Graham Association

Box 1240, Minneapolis, MN 55440

Why sayest thou, O Jacob, and speakest, O Israel, My way is hid from the Lord, and my judgment is passed over from my God? Hast thou not known, hast thou not heard, that the everlasting God, the Lord, the Creator of the ends of the earth, fainteth not, neither is weary? there is no searching of his understanding. He giveth power to the faint; and to them that have no might he increaseth strength (Isaiah 40:27–29).

When we say with Jacob, "My way is hid from the Lord," it is because we do not know God. He is hidden from us, and we think He is therefore absent; we do not see Him, and we think He does not see us. Like a child in dilirium, that cannot see its mother, although she is holding it tenderly in her arms, and that calls out in despair, "O Mother, Mother, come!" so we in the delirium of our unbelief call out, "How long wilt Thou forget me, O Lord? Forever? How long wilt Thou hide Thy face from me?" while all the time His arms are underneath us, and His love environs us on every side.

If I say, Surely the darkness shall cover me; even the night shall be light about me. Yea, the darkness hideth not from thee; but the night shineth as the day: the darkness and the light are both alike to thee (Psalms 139:11, 12).

God may be hidden from us, but we can never be hidden from Him. There is a scene in the life of Elisha that illustrates this. The King of Syria was warring against Israel, but his designs were continually frustrated by Elisha. At last he determined to take Elisha captive, and sent an army to surround the prophet's own city. I will let the Bible tell the rest of the story.

And when the servant of the man of God was risen early, and gone forth, behold, an host compassed the city both with horses and chariots. And his servant said unto him, Alas, my master! how shall we do? And he answered, Fear not: for they that be with us are more than they that be with them. And Elisha prayed, and said, Lord, I pray thee, open his eyes, that he may see. And the Lord opened the eyes of the young man; and he saw: and, behold, the mountain was full of horses and chariots of fire round about Elisha (2 Kings 6:15–17).

Were our eyes but opened, as were the eyes of this young man, we too should see, in every time of trial or danger, the mountains round about us full of the horses and chariots of God!

And, behold, two of them went that same day to a village called Emmaus, which was from Jerusalem about threescore furlongs. And they talked together of all these things which had happened. And it came to pass, that, while they communed together and reasoned, Jesus himself drew near, and went with them. But their eyes were holden that they should not know him (Luke 24:13–16).

Now as then it often happens that the Lord is walking with His people, as He did with the two disciples on their way to Emmaus, and like them, we do not know Him. We need to have our eyes opened that we may see Him. These disciples saw with their bodily eyes, but we are to see with our spiritual eyes. Our seeing is to be by believing. Faith is the soul's eyesight. The word *see* is used not only of the sense of vision by which we perceive external objects, but also of that inward perception which gives us a certain knowledge of spiritual things. We say, for instance, of a mathematical problem, "I see it," meaning, not that our outward eyes see it worked out on a blackboard, but that our inward perception grasps it as an ascertained fact. It is in this sense that we shall come to see Him who is invisible, not with our outward eyes, but with the inward eye of our deepest perceptions. In other words, if we would discover the hidden God, we must simply believe, in spite of every "seeming" to the contrary, that He is with us and is watching over us and caring for us every minute of the time. Though we see Him not, we must believe He is there, and, so believing, we shall surely "rejoice with joy unspeakable and full of glory!"

Whom having not seen, ye love; in whom, though now ye see him not, yet believing, ye rejoice with joy unspeakable and full of glory: Receiving the end of your faith, even the salvation of your souls (1 Peter 1:8, 9).

> My child went forth into my garden-fair,
>   Having no wish nor will to stay by me;
> But that I patiently had followed him out there
>   He could not see.
>
> He passed on from the garden to the wild,
>   Where cruel and fierce-roaring monsters lie;
> I drove them back, but nothing told the child
>   That it was I.

He saw his brothers toiling on the road,
  "I will give life and strength for them," cried he;
But that I made him strong to lift their load
    He did not see.

Soul-thrilling words of love bade him rejoice,
  And filled with music all that desert place;
And yet he never knew it was my voice,
    Nor saw my face.

And when the night came and his eyes grew dim,
  And dark and chill and mists about him lay,
He did not know my hand was guiding him,
    Till it was day.

Lesson 11

No Thing *Versus* All Things

FOUNDATION TEXT:—Having nothing, and yet possessing all things.—2 Corinthians 6:10.

The Apostle Paul gives us this paradox as one of the foundation principles of the Christian life: having nothing, or, as it may be translated, no thing, and yet possessing all things. It is a saying of the deepest significance, for it strikes a blow at the whole fabric of the ordinary Christian life. The ambition of most Christians, so far from being an ambition to have nothing, is, on the contrary, an ambition to have a vast number of things; and their energies are all wasted in the vain effort to get possession of these things. Some strive to get possession of certain "experiences"; some seek after "ecstatic feelings"; some try to make themselves rich in theological "views" and "dogmas"; some store up a long list of works done and results achieved; some seek to acquire "illuminations," or to accumulate "gifts" and "graces." In short, all Christians, almost without exception, seek to possess a store of something or other, which they fancy will serve to recommend them to God, and make them worthy of His love and care. Could we but understand clearly the meaning of Paul's words, "having nothing, yet possessing all things," all this would be at an end. For we would see that the one thing God wants of us is that we should empty ourselves of all our own things, in order that we may be brought to depend on Him for everything; we should discover that His purpose is to bring us to the place where we have nothing apart from Himself.

And the Lord spake unto Aaron, Thou shalt have no inheritance in their land, neither shalt thou have any part among them: I am thy part and thine inheritance among the children of Israel (Numbers 18:20).

But unto the tribe of Levi Moses gave not any inheritance: the Lord God of Israel was their inheritance, as he said unto them (Joshua 13:33).

"I am thine inheritance!" What an amazing saying! No wonder the Levites were content to go without any other possessions! Having nothing, they truly possessed all things, for God was their possession! How slow we are to see that this is our privilege now, just as really as it was that of the Levites in those days of old. Apart from Christ we, in fact, have nothing; for moth and rust are sure to corrupt, and thieves to break through and steal all merely human possessions. But if God is ours, then all things are eternally ours, for what belongs to God must of necessity belong to us also, according to our need and our measure.

He that spared not his own Son, but delivered him up for us all, how shall he not with him also freely give us all things (Romans 8:32).

Blessed be the God and Father of our Lord Jesus Christ, who hath blessed us with all spiritual blessings in heavenly places in Christ (Ephesians 1:3).

It is here declared that all things have been given to us freely in Christ, but as a matter of fact we may not yet ourselves have taken possession of all. When our hands are full of our own things, we cannot possibly get possession of the things of God. Only empty hands can grasp a gift, only empty vessels can receive the filling; and only the heart that is emptied of all its own things can receive the "all things" of God. I mean, for instance, that if Christians are enjoying very ecstatic "experiences" they cannot help resting in them, and will feel no need to find their rest in God alone. Therefore it is that God finds it so often necessary to take away all our own things, and to leave us empty and bereft of all that we have most valued. He dries up our "fervours," He deadens our "feelings"; He spoils our "experiences"; He confuses our "views," He clouds our "illuminations"; and so brings us at last to the place where, having nothing of our own, we are driven to find our rest in the "all things" of God. I believe this is the explanation of the dark and perplexing dispensations through which many of God's children are called to pass, when they seem to have lost all the joy and clearness of their earlier experiences, and to have been plunged into a fog of darkness and distress. Did they but understand it, they would give God thanks that, in His tender love, He is thus depriving them of all their own possessions; since it is only so that He can bring them safely and surely to the place where they will be content to possess Himself alone. "Having nothing," they will at last "possess all things."

The Bible exhorts us not to glory in our wisdom, or our might, or our riches, even though we may be possessed of all three; but, "let him that glorieth, glory in this, that he understandeth and knoweth the Lord."

Have we any of us ever come to the place where we have honestly ceased to glory in our own possessions? Never, I believe, until we have been deprived of them. Human nature is so constituted that while it possesses anything, it can hardly help glorying in it. As long, for instance, as a Christian feels wise or strong or rich in spiritual things, that Christian will almost inevitably glory in his strength, or his wisdom, or his riches. But if these are taken away from him, he will be driven to glory in the Lord alone, simply because there will be nothing else for him to glory in.

> Ho, every one that thirsteth, come ye to the waters, and he that hath no money; come ye, buy and eat; yea, come, buy wine and milk without money and without price. Wherefore do ye spend money for that which is not bread? and your labour for that which satisfieth not? hearken diligently unto me, and eat ye that which is good, and let your soul delight itself in fatness (Isaiah 55:1, 2).

The sharp contrast here drawn between our things and God's things is very striking. Our things all partake of the nature of "that which is not bread" and "that which satisfieth not." They are of the earth, earthy; and consequently cannot, in the very nature of things, satisfy the spirit that is from heaven.

> Labour not for the meat which perisheth, but for that meat which endureth unto everlasting life, which the Son of man shall give unto you: for him hath God the Father sealed (John 6:27).

Everything that can perish belongs to the sphere of earthly things. Experiences perish, feelings perish, views perish, doctrines perish; the Apostle tells us that prophecies fail, and tongues cease, and knowledge vanishes away. It is impossible, therefore, that any of these perishable things, no matter how good of their kind they may be, could really satisfy the imperishable spirit. But while we labor for and hold on to the perishable things, we shall have no energy to seek after, nor room to hold the "meat which endureth unto everlasting life."

I do not mean by this that the soul ought not to have any experiences, or views, or doctrines, or knowledge, or strength. Paul had all these in greater measure, I suppose, than anyone else ever had, and yet he could declare that he had "nothing." What he meant was that he had nothing apart from Christ, but that he had all things in Christ. That is, Christ was his strength and wisdom and righteousness, and in himself he had nothing. I know this is a little difficult to explain. The illustration that helps me the most, though even this is not perfect, is that of the steam working through the machinery. The machinery has no power of its own, but all its power is derived from the steam that works through it and by it. Could the machinery speak, its language would be similar to Paul's, "having nothing, and yet possessing all things."

> For it is God which worketh in you both to will and to do of his good pleasure (Philippians 2:13).
> But God hath chosen the foolish things of the world to confound the wise; and God hath chosen the weak things of the world to confound the things which are mighty; And base things of the world, and things which are despised, hath God chosen, yea, and things which are not, to bring to nought things that are: That no flesh should glory in his presence. But of him are ye in Christ Jesus, who of God is made unto us wisdom, and righteousness, and sanctification, and redemption: That, according as it is written, He that glorifieth, let him glory in the Lord (1 Corinthians 1:27–31).

We must lay aside our own wisdom and righeousness in order that Christ may be made wisdom and righteousness and sanctification unto us. Practically, this means, that if I want righteousness of any kind I must not try to get a store of it laid up within myself, but must draw my supplies of righteousness moment by moment from the Lord, as I need it. I remember once when I felt the need of a great stock of patience to meet an emergency that was coming upon me, and thought I would be obliged to pray for a long time in order to lay up enough. I think I expected to have something after the nature of a package of patience, done up and labeled "Patience," and deposited in my heart. It was one night, and I was preparing myself to pray all night long in order to lay in a good supply, when suddenly this verse flashed into my mind, "Who of God is made unto us wisdom, and righteousness, and sanctification, and redemption." "Yes," I added with a sudden illumination, "and patience too! I do not need to lay up a stock of patience; all the patience I need is stored up for me in Christ, and I have only to draw my supplies momentarily from Him." I rose from my knees at once, and thanked the Lord beforehand for the unlimited supply of patience that I saw was mine in Christ. And I need not say that I found grace (in the form of patience) to help in every time of need.

Does not common sense tell us that, if we may thus have the "all things" of God, it is the height of folly to want to keep our own things, poor and good for nothing, as they necessarily are? Was it not simple good common sense on Paul's part to count all things but loss compared to the excellency of the knowledge of Christ?

> But what things were gain to me, those I counted loss for Christ. Yea doubtless, and I count all things but loss for the excellency of the knowledge of Christ Jesus my Lord: for whom I have suffered the loss of all things, and do count them but dung, that I may win Christ (Philippians 3:7, 8).

The loss of all things meant to Paul the gain of all things. The loss of the nest to the young eaglet, who is just learning to fly, means the gain of the whole heavens for its home. The loss of our own strength means the gaining of God's strength in its place; the loss of our own wisdom means the gaining of God's wisdom; the loss of our own life means the gaining of God's life. Who would not make the exchange?

> There is that maketh himself rich, yet hath nothing: there is that maketh himself poor, yet hath great riches (Proverbs 13:7).

To which of these two classes do we belong? Are we seeking to make ourselves rich, or are we content to be poor and possess nothing? I used to have a friend who talked a great deal about what she called the "stripping chamber." She was one of those who are continually trying to "make themselves rich" by seeking after "experiences" and "blessings," and she could not seem to understand why the Lord found it necessary so continually to strip her of all that she had gained. An old writer, in a little book called *The Saint's Travel to the Land of Canaan,* thus describes this stripping process:

"God in these days is discovering the false coverings of creatures, and so stripping them naked. He is bringing men to see the great mystery of self in all its supposed glory. He is annihilating creatures, and bringing them to a spiritual death. He is laying low mountains, and is unbottoming creatures from their false rests. Men's lofty looks He is abasing; yea, He is bringing men, who have been as it were Stars, and of great account in their own and in others' eyes, even to a loss and silence, confusion and darkness; so that now their light seems to be darkness, their wisdom folly, their life death; and their enlargements and self-actings are hedged up, and they cannot find out any of their former paths. And all this is that the creature may be brought to depend on the Creator, and have nothing apart from Him."

I believe many will realize that they have been taken at times into this same "stripping chamber," and have known something of this stripping work of God. Perhaps hitherto it may have frightened and perplexed them; but, henceforth, if they only understand it aright, they will rejoice at every stripping that deprives them of their own things, and that brings them to the place where, having nothing of their own, they can possess all things in God.

> And it shall be unto them for an inheritance: I am their inheritance: and ye shall give them no possession in Israel: I am their possession (Ezekiel 44:28).

Contrast the "no possession" here with the "I am their possession," and we shall get a faint glimpse perhaps of what it means to have nothing, and yet possess all things.

> So likewise, whosoever he be of you that forsaketh not all that he hath, he cannot be my disciple (Luke 14:33).
> Then answered Peter and said unto him, Behold we have forsaken all, and followed thee; what shall we have therefore? And Jesus said unto them, Verily I say unto you, That ye which have followed me, in the regeneration when the Son of man shall sit in the throne of his

glory, ye also shall sit upon twelve thrones, judging the twelve tribes of Israel. And every one that hath forsaken houses, or brethren, or sisters, or father, or mother, or wife, or children, or lands, for my name's sake, shall receive an hundredfold, and shall inherit everlasting life (Matthew 19:27–29).

All that we have, whether outward or inward, must be "forsaken," if we would receive the hundredfold of God. Forsaken, not in the sense of literally getting rid of everything, but in the sense of having everything only in and from the Lord. The real facts of the case are, that only God knows how to take care of things as they ought to be taken care of, and He alone is able to do it; therefore the common sense of the matter is that nothing is really safe until it is handed over to His care. The most unsafe person in the universe to have charge of my things is myself; and never do I possess them so firmly as when I have transferred them over into the hands of God, and have left them in His charge. Never am I so sure of my money as when I have transferred it out of my unsafe pockets into the safe custody of a trustworthy bank; and the same thing is true as regards the abandonment of all I possess into the custody of God. It may be considered a very pious thing to do this, but it certainly is only good common sense as well.

Therefore if any man be in Christ, he is a new creature: old things are passed away; behold, all things are become new. And all things are of God, who hath reconciled us to himself by Jesus Christ, and hath given to us the ministry of reconciliation (2 Corinthians 5:17, 18).

The "old things," here spoken of as "passing away," are everything that belongs to the "old man" or the carnal or fleshly life; the old activities of the flesh, the old efforts to generate for self something in a religious way to recommend us to God, the old way of relying on "exercises" and "ordinances" and "duties" of various kinds, to beget and feed the life of God in the soul. Those who have been born into the resurrection life must learn that none of these things are of any avail in the sphere upon which they have entered. Here all things must be of God; and the old things of the flesh must vanish to make room for the new things of God.

Wherefore if ye be dead with Christ from the rudiments of the world, why, as though living in the world, are ye subject to ordinances (Touch not; taste not; Handle not; Which all are to perish with the using;) after the commandments and doctrines of men? Which things have indeed a shew of wisdom in will worship, and humility, and neglecting of the body; not in any honour to the satisfying of the flesh. If ye then be risen with Christ, seek those things which are above, where Christ sitteth on the right hand of God. Set your affection on things above, not on things on the earth. For ye are dead, and your life is hid with Christ in God (Colossians 2:20–23; 3:1–3).

Our things, that is, our feelings, our experiences, our exercises of various sorts, seem often to have a "show of wisdom," and it is hard for us to count them as really nothing, and to say truly, when we seem to have so many things, that we have nothing. But anything that is what the Apostle calls "rudiments of the world," that is, anything that is wrought out by "flesh" in any way whatever, must always be "nothing" in the sight of God; and, as soon as we have learned to see things with His eyes, they will be nothing in our own sight also. The commonsense way in everything always is to get down to facts, and in this case the simple fact is that all our own possessions of any kind whatsoever are literally and truly "nothing," and that, no matter how many we may have of them, we still must say with the Apostle, if we speak the truth, "having nothing."

For we brought nothing into this world, and it is certain we can carry nothing out (1 Timothy 6:7).

Whether we can go on and say further with the Apostle, "that although we have nothing, we yet possess all things," depends upon how much we believe of the Scripture declarations that all things are ours in Christ. Not will be, notice, but are ours now. That is, precisely as what the mother has belongs to the child at its need, so what God has belongs to His children at their need, and only awaits their taking.

According as his divine power hath given unto us all things that pertain unto life and godliness, through the knowledge of him that hath called us to glory and virtue (2 Peter 1:3).
Therefore let no man glory in men. For all things are yours; Whether Paul, or Apollos, or Cephas, or the world, or life, or death, or things present, or things to come; all are yours; And ye are Christ's; and Christ is God's (1 Corinthians 3:21–23).

Lord, in thy Spirit's hurricane, I pray,
Strip my soul naked, dress it then thy way.
Change for me all my rags to cloth of gold.
Who would not poverty for riches yield?
A hovel sell to buy a treasure-field?
Who would a mess of porridge careful hold
Against the universe's birthright old?

Taking Up the Cross

FOUNDATION TEXT:—Then said Jesus unto his disciples, If any man will come after me, let him deny himself, and take up his cross, and follow me. For whosoever will save his life shall lose it: and whosoever will lose his life for my sake shall find it.—Matthew 16:24, 25.

A great deal of misunderstanding exists in regard to this subject of "taking up the cross." Most people think it means doing the will of God under a feeling of great trial; giving up something that we very much want to keep, or performing some duty from which we exceedingly shrink. Consequently we often hear the expression used in reference to some act of obedience to what is thought to be the will of God, "Well, I suppose I must take up my cross and do it"; and the long face and accompanying sigh testify to how "heavy" this cross is felt to be. Now, I believe all this falls far short of what our Lord really meant when He said, "If any man will come after me, let him deny himself, and take up his cross and follow me." It is inconceivable to me that He could have meant that doing the will of God was to be a hard yoke and a heavy burden to the child of God. In fact, He Himself declared exactly the opposite, when He said that His yoke was easy and His burden light. Taking up the cross, therefore, cannot mean that it is to be hard to do God's will; and I believe a careful study of the subject will show us that it has a far deeper and wider signification.

As far as I can see, the cross in Scripture always means death.

And being found in fashion as a man, he humbled himself, and became obedient unto death, even the death of the cross (Philippians 2:8).

111

And that he might reconcile both unto God in one body by the cross, having slain the enmity thereby (Ephesians 2:16).

The cross in connection with Christ always means the death of Christ. The only use of the cross is to put to death, not to keep alive. It may be a suffering death, but still it is sooner or later death. All through the Bible the meaning of the cross is simply and always death. In most cases this is manifest to everyone; and why we have chosen to give it a different meaning in its mystical sense, and make it mean not death, but a living in misery, would be hard to explain. When, therefore, our Lord told His disciples that they could not be His disciples unless they took up the cross, He could not have meant that they were to find it hard to do His will; but He was, I believe, simply expressing in figurative language the fact that they were to be made partakers of His death and resurrection, by having their old man crucified with Him, and by living only in their new man, or, in other words, in the resurrection life of the Spirit.

Knowing this, that our old man is crucified with him, that the body of sin might be destroyed, that henceforth we should not serve sin (Romans 6:6).

But God forbid that I should glory, save in the cross of our Lord Jesus Christ, by whom the world is crucified unto me, and I unto the world. For in Christ Jesus neither circumcision availeth any thing, nor uncircumcision, but a new creature (Galatians 6:14, 15).

Many people seem to think that the only thing proposed in religion is to improve the "old man," that is, the flesh; and that the way to do this is to discipline and punish it until it is compelled to behave. Hence comes the asceticism of the Buddhist and others; and hence, also, comes the idea that the "cross" for Christians consists in the painful struggles of this helpless "old man" to do the will of God, a will which in the very nature of things the flesh cannot understand or love. But a true comprehension of the religion of Christ shows us that what is really meant is the death of this old man and the birth in us of a "new creature," begotten of God, whose tastes and instincts are all in harmony with God, and to whom the doing of God's will must be, and cannot help being, a joy and a delight. It is not the old man thwarted and made miserable, by being compelled to submit to a will it dislikes, but it is a new man, "created in Christ Jesus unto good works," and therefore doing these good works with ease and pleasure; a new nature, of divine origin, which is in harmony with the divine will, and therefore delights to do it.

> Therefore if any man be in Christ, he is a new creature: old things are passed away; behold, all things are become new. And all things are of God . . . (2 Corinthians 5:17, 18; also Ephesians 4:22–24).

The "new creature" does not mean a new body, of a new intellect, but a new spirit, a new life. It means that the man who has become a new creature has had implanted within him the life principle of a new and spiritual nature, the life and nature of God. He is made a "partaker of the Divine nature." It is not his old fleshly nature made better, but a new and higher nature introduced; a nature belonging to a higher order of being. It is a life born of the Spirit, in contradistinction to the life born of the flesh.

> That which is born of the flesh is flesh; and that which is born of the Spirit is spirit (John 3:6).
> And so it is written, The first man Adam was made a living soul; the last Adam was made a quickening spirit. Howbeit that was not first which is spiritual, but that which is natural; and afterward that which is spiritual. The first man is of the earth, earthy; the second man is the Lord from heaven. As is the earthy, such are they also that are earthy: and as is the heavenly, such are they also that are heavenly. And as we have borne the image of the earthy, we shall also bear the image of the heavenly (1 Corinthians 15:45–49).

That which is born of the flesh is flesh, and never can be anything else, no matter how much we discipline it. The only way to treat it is to nail it to the cross; or, in other words, put it to death; not keep it alive to make it suffer, but crucify it, that is, kill it, and let it be to us as a dead and buried thing.

> And they that are Christ's have crucified the flesh with the affections and lusts (Galatians 5:24).

To crucify, means to put to death, not to keep alive in misery. But so obscured has the whole subject become to the children of God, that I believe a great many feel as if they were crucifying self when they are simply seating self on a pinnacle, and are tormenting it and making it miserable. Man will undergo the most painful self-sacrifices, and call it "taking up the cross," and will find great satisfaction in it; and all the time will fail to understand that the true cross consists in counting the flesh, or the "old man," as an utterly worthless thing, fit only to be put to death. There is a subtle enjoyment in torturing the outward self, if only the interior self-life may be fed thereby. A man will make himself a fakir, if it is only self that does it, so that self can share in the glory. The flesh of man likes to have some credit; it cannot bear to be counted as dead and therefore ignored; and in all religions of legality it has a chance. This explains, I am sure, why there is so much legality among Christians. But did we read the Scriptures aright, we should see that the carnal mind, that is, the fleshly mind (as it is literally translated), cannot serve God nor enter into His kingdom, no matter how much we may try, by all sorts of asceticism, to make it fit.

> For they that are after the flesh do mind the things of the flesh; but they that are after the Spirit the things of the Spirit. For to be carnally minded is death; but to be spiritually minded is life and peace. Because the carnal mind is enmity against God: for it is not subject to the law of God, neither indeed can be. So then they that are in the flesh cannot please God (Romans 8:5–8).

When the Apostle says here that they who are "in the flesh" cannot please God, it is manifest he cannot mean, that they who are in the body cannot please God, for it is to people in the body that all his exhortations are addressed. The "flesh" here, therefore, must mean the lower nature in man, that part of his nature that is called "the carnal mind, or the old Adam." It is the part of man's being that must die in order that the "new man" or the spiritual nature may be born. If a caterpillar is to become a butterfly, the only way is for the caterpillar life to die in order that the butterfly life may be evolved. And just as the caterpillar cannot live the butterfly life, so also the "flesh" or "carnal nature" in us cannot live the spiritual life. It is in this sense that Paul says he is crucified with Christ.

> I am crucified with Christ: nevertheless I live; yet not I, but Christ liveth in me; and the life which I now live in the flesh I live by the faith of the Son of God, who loved me, and gave himself for me (Galatians 2:20).
> But God forbid that I should glory, save in the cross of our Lord Jesus Christ, by whom the world is crucified unto me, and I unto the world (Galatians 6:14).

By being "crucified to the world" Paul meant that he was dead to it. He did not mean that he was still alive to it, and was being made to suffer because he must give it up, but that he was absolutely dead to it, so that it no longer had any attractions for him. To be dead to a thing must mean that that thing has no power to attract. And this is what is meant in the Bible by "taking up the cross." It is to become so dead to the world (that is, the lower plane of living) that its power to tempt is gone. It is to have our affections so set on things above, that merely earthly things have lost their charm.

If ye then be risen with Christ, seek those things which are above, where Christ sitteth on the right hand of God. Set your affection on things above, not on things on the earth. For ye are dead, and your life is hid with Christ in God (Colossians 3:1–3).

To have our "affections set" on anything must mean that we love that thing; and if our affections are set on the will of God, we must love His will. It is impossible that God's will should seem hard to a man whose affections are set on it. It may be accompanied with hard things, but in itself it must be a delight. Our Lord could say, "I delight to do thy will, O my God!" because He was dead to everything that was contrary to His Father's will. His affections were set on the will of God; and until our affections are similarly so set on the will of God as to delight in it, we have not "taken up the cross" in the Scripture sense at all.

A good illustration of what I mean would be the change that takes place in the feelings of a little girl when she becomes a woman. As a child she loved to roll hoops, and climb trees, and make mud pies; and she hated to sit still and sew, or to learn long lessons, or to do hard work. To have been compelled to give up the one or to do the other, while still a child, would have been a bitter trial. But when the little girl becomes a woman, everything is reversed, and she loves the things she once hated, and hates the things she once loved. The woman "takes up the cross" to her childish plays; that is, she becomes dead to them, and no longer finds any pleasure in them. She delights in the pursuits of maturity and scorns the pursuits of childhood, just as once she delighted in the pursuits of childhood and scorned those of maturity.

I fear there are a great many Christians who look upon the Christian life, as I in my childish ignorance looked upon grown-up life. I thought that grown-up people wanted to play as much as I did, but that there was a law forbidding it after a certain age; and I pitied with all my heart everybody who had passed that age, which, somehow, I fixed in my mind at fifteen, and dreaded beyond measure the time when I should reach that age myself, and should have to "take up the cross" that awaited me there. In the same way I believe many Christians think religion means always to give up the things they love, and to do the things they hate; and they call this "taking up the cross," and actually think God enjoys this "grudging" service.

> Every man according as he purposeth in his heart, so let him give; not grudgingly, or of necessity: for God loveth a cheerful giver (2 Corinthians 9:7).

To my mind, grudging service is no more acceptable to God from us than it would be to us from one another; and such an idea of the "cross" as this, seems to me a very poor and low substitute for the glorious truth of our death with Christ, and our resurrection into the triumphant spiritual life hid with Christ in God. Surely, if we are born of God, we must love the things God loves, and hate the things He hates; and if we are one with Christ, it is out of the question that we should chafe against His will or find His service hard! Is it a sign of the highest sort of union between a husband and wife when the one finds it a great trial to please the other? Ought it not rather to be a joy to do so? And how much more is this true as regards our relations to Christ?

> Always bearing about in the body the dying of the Lord Jesus, that the life also of Jesus might be made manifest in our body. For we which live are alway delivered unto death for Jesus' sake, that the life also of Jesus might be made manifest in our mortal flesh (2 Corinthians 4:10, 11).

Dying and *death* are very definite words, and can only mean that that which is said to be "crucified," and is therefore called dead, must be in a condition spiritually analogous to what death is physically, that is, without life, or feeling, or capacity to suffer. Therefore, to such the doing of God's will cannot cause suffering, for the simple reason that that part of their being which dislikes God's will and shrinks from doing it, is dead, and only that part is alive that loves God's will and delights to do it.

> Likewise reckon ye also yourselves to be dead indeed unto sin, but alive unto God through Jesus Christ our Lord. Let not sin therefore reign in your mortal body, that ye should obey it in the lusts thereof. Neither yield ye your members as instruments of unrighteousness unto sin: but yield yourselves unto God, as those that are alive from the dead, and your members as instruments of righteousness unto God (Romans 6:11-13).

"Reckoning ourselves to be dead indeed unto sin" is only another expression for "taking up our cross and denying ourselves." It simply means that we are to look upon ourselves as dead to the things of the flesh that once attracted us, and as alive only to the higher things of God. Or, in other words, we are to live in the higher part of our nature instead of in the lower. There are always two attitudes of mind towards anything, between which we may choose. Either we may take hold of things on the plane of flesh, or we may take hold of them on the plane of spirit; and it is to do the latter that the Apostle exhorts us when he tells us to reckon ourselves "alive unto God."

> And ye are complete in him, which is the head of all principality and power: In whom also ye are circumcised with the circumcision made without hands, in putting off the body of the sins of the flesh by the circumcision of Christ: Buried with him in baptism, wherein also ye are risen with him through the faith of the operation of God, who hath raised him from the dead (Colossians 2:10-12).

Certainly a thing that is "buried" cannot be at the same time alive to suffering. Paul's whole argument in the sixth of Romans is founded on this.

> What shall we say then? Shall we continue in sin, that grace may abound? God forbid. How shall we that are dead to sin, live any longer therein? Know ye not, that so many of us as were baptized into Jesus Christ were baptized into his death? Therefore we are buried with him by baptism into death: that like as Christ was raised up from the dead by the glory of the Father, even so we also should walk in newness of life (Romans 6:1-4).

He does not say we ought not to sin, which might imply that secretly we wanted to, but were restrained by certain considerations;

but he says, "we are dead to sin, and therefore we cannot sin," that is, we do not want to. This, I think, is what John means in that passage in his Epistle which some find so difficult.

> Whosoever is born of God doth not commit sin; for his seed remaineth in him: and he cannot sin, because he is born of God (1 John 3:9).

That part of us which is born of God, the spiritual man in us, cannot sin, because it is holy in its very nature or essence. If we sin, therefore, it must be because we have permitted that in us which is born of the flesh to have some life; and have submitted ourselves, that is, our personality, more or less to its control. And not only would I say this concerning sin, but I would also say it concerning that shrinking from and dislike of God's will which so many Christians think constitutes the cross. The spiritual man in us cannot dislike God's will, for in the very nature of things that which is born of God must love the will of God. That which shrinks therefore and suffers, must be the self-life; and the self-life we are commanded to crucify and deny (Mark 8:34, 35).

To deny anything means that you do not recognize its existence. To deny ourselves therefore does not mean to keep self alive, and let it be made miserable by forcing it to do God's will; but it means to deny the very existence of self, and to live only in that part of our nature that loves God's will and delights to do it. We can see what the Scriptures mean by denying, if we refer to the story of Peter (*see* Matthew 26:34, 35; 69–75).

Peter simply said, "I know not the man," and this was denying Christ. And similarly if we would deny self, we must say to self, "I do not know you." Fénelon tells us that the true self-denial consists in looking upon this "I," of whom we are all so fond, as a stranger in whom we take no interest. "I do not know you," we must say. "You may be the most interesting or the most ill-used person in the world, but you need not bring your tales to me, for you are a stranger to me, and I take no interest in you." If anyone objects that it is not possible to lose all interest in self after this fashion, I would ask them, if they have never known what it was to be so overmastered by some strong emotion of love, or of joy, or of sorrow, as to forget and deny self utterly, and not even to notice what happens to it? We say at such times, "I entirely forgot myself," and what is this but to deny self in the most effectual sort of way?

> Therefore I take pleasure in infirmities, in reproaches, in necessities, in persecutions, in distresses for Christ's sake: for when I am weak, then am I strong (2 Corinthians 12:10).

The Apostle did not look upon his trials as a heavy "cross," hard to be borne, but he "took pleasure" in them. He had so effectually taken up the true cross by which he was "crucified to the world," as to delight in the will of God, even when it involved trials and persecutions, and distresses and necessities.

The true lover takes pleasure in suffering, if need be, for the one he loves; and if we love our Lord, it is not anything very mystical for us to "take pleasure" in suffering endured for His sake.

This seems to me simple common sense; and although we may not all have attained to it, yet it is of the utmost importance that we should not hinder our advance thitherward by cherishing false notions of what we are called to as children of God, and by degrading the grand Scripture idea of denying ourselves and taking up our cross, to the poor paltry fact of being compelled to give up things we love, and to do things we dislike. If things are wrong we ought to hate them, and want to give them up; and if duties are right, we ought to love them, and delight to do them. And we shall do this, if we have truly "taken up our cross," and are indeed "crucified with Christ."

I know these expressions, "crucified with Christ," and "dead to sin," are looked upon as being very mysterious and occult; and simpleminded Christians think they describe experiences that but few can comprehend or attain to. But whatever mystical meaning they may have, there is a practical commonsense meaning as well, that the most simpleminded can understand. They mean just what is meant by the ordinary expression of being "dead" to anything. For instance, I suppose all my readers are "dead" to stealing or murder; that is, they do not want to commit either of these crimes. They are "crucified to the world" as regards these sins, and no doubt as regards many others. They have "taken up the cross" to them. Now, there is nothing mysterious or occult in this common experience, and it will serve as a sample of what the Bible means when it tells us we must "take up the cross" and be "crucified with Christ." It means simply this, that, just as now we have "taken up the cross" to some of the things that are contrary to the will of God, and are "dead" to them, so must we henceforth "take up the cross," and be "dead" to all that is opposed to His will.

The Law of Faith

FOUNDATION TEXT:—Where is boasting then? It is excluded. By what law? of works? Nay: but by the law of faith.—Romans 3:27.

In considering this text not long ago, it dawned upon me that the expression, the "law of faith," must have a deeper meaning than is sometimes given to it. The word *law* emphasized itself to my mind, and I saw it could not mean only the fact of faith, or the results of faith; but that it must also mean the law by which faith works, its inherent nature as it were, or its mode of action. We speak of the law of gravitation, or the law of chemical affinities, and we mean something far more than the mere facts or phenomena of gravitation or chemical affinities. We mean the laws behind the facts, which govern the facts, and which are their mode of working.

The law which lies behind the fact is, of course, the really potent thing. The fact of gravitation was a great discovery, but it would not have revolutionized the world as it has without the further discovery of its laws. Until these laws were discovered, the mighty force hidden in the fact of gravitation was comparatively worthless. It could not be applied.

We have nothing here to do with the doctrines concerning faith. These are for theologians. But what we need is to get at the practical commonsense everyday laws of the spiritual life, that we may use them in our daily battle with the world.

The progress of thought and investigation removes all things in the material world, sooner or later, out of the region of isolated and unexplained fact, into the region of ascertained and orderly law; the region where whatever powers they may possess become capable of practical application.

Something of this same progress of thought in regard to faith may be seen in the spiritual world. The facts of faith have been brought before Christians of late years with increasing prominence. We have had Faith Missions, and Faith Homes, and Faith Healing, and Faith Works in abundance, and the Church has gradually been learning that faith is a real and mighty spiritual force, which can accomplish things and control things in a way that cannot be accounted for except on the ground of some actual definite *law* of faith, that works with the irresistible and inevitable certainty of all law in every region of life.

> And he said unto her, Daughter, thy faith hath made thee whole; go in peace, and be whole of thy plague (Mark 5:34).
> And he said unto him, Arise, go thy way: thy faith hath made thee whole" (Luke 17:19).
> And he said to the woman, Thy faith hath saved thee; go in peace (Luke 7:50).
> Then touched he their eyes, saying, According to your faith be it unto you (Matthew 9:29).

We are all familiar with these declarations of our Lord, and have all repeated many a time to ourselves and to others the magical words, "According to your faith" it shall be unto you. But have we not looked upon them too much as magical words, involving a sort of continuous miracle, for which there was no law, and about which there could be no certainty? Has not the feeling concerning faith been more or less that it is a capricious, uncertain factor, which may work or may not, and upon which no real dependence can ever be placed? Has not the exercise of it been always somewhat of an experiment, even with the most devout souls? And is not the wonder and admiration with which we regard a successful issue to its ventures, an indication that the truth has hardly yet dawned upon us of a "law of faith," about whose working there can be no experiment and no doubt?

> Jesus answered and said unto them, Verily I say unto you, If ye have faith, and doubt not, ye shall not only do this which is done to the fig tree, but also if ye shall say unto this mountain, Be thou removed, and

be thou cast into the sea; it shall be done. And all things whatsoever ye shall ask in prayer, believing, ye shall receive (Matthew 21:21, 22).

There is no experiment or doubt in the faith here described. It is an assertion of the most uncompromising nature, that there is a "law of faith" which will inevitably work, wherever and whenever it is applied, and that not even mountains can withstand it.

> And the Lord said, If ye had faith as a grain of mustard seed, ye might say unto this sycamine tree, Be thou plucked up by the root, and be thou planted in the sea; and it should obey you (Luke 17:6).
>
> Then came the disciples to Jesus apart, and said, Why could not we cast him out? And Jesus said unto them, Because of your unbelief: for verily I say unto you, If ye have faith as a grain of mustard seed, ye shall say unto this mountain, Remove hence to yonder place; and it shall remove; and nothing shall be impossible unto you (Matthew 17:19, 20).

All these astounding assertions are from the lips of our Lord Himself, and they must contain a deeper truth than any the Church has yet comprehended, or our achievements in the region of faith could not possibly be so few and meager. I believe myself that Christ was here telling us of a mighty, irresistible, spiritual law, that is inherent in the nature of God, and that is shared, according to our measure, by everyone who is begotten of God, and is a partaker of His divine nature. Just as gravitation is a law of matter, inherent in matter, and absolutely unerring and unintermittent in its working, so is faith a law of spirit, inherent in spirit, and equally unerring and unintermittent in its working. When Christ says, therefore, that "nothing shall be impossible" to faith, He is not stating a marvelous fact only, but He is revealing a tremendous law.

> Jesus said unto him, If thou canst believe, all things are possible to him that believeth (Mark 9:23).

We know that all things are possible to God, and here our Lord tells us that all things are possible to us also, if we only believe. No assertion could be more distinct or unmistakable. The great thing for us, therefore, is to discover the law by which faith works, in order that we may know how to exercise this tremendous spiritual force, that is declared by our Lord to be our birthright, as being children of God, and partakers of His nature.

First of all, then, let us consider what faith is not, that we may be better able to understand what it really is.

By very many faith is considered to be a gracious disposition of the soul, wrought by the Holy Ghost in answer to wrestling prayer, which puts us in a fit condition to receive favors from God. By others it is thought to be an acceptable frame of mind, that causes God to be pleased with us. Others look upon faith as though it were a sort of *thing,* received also in answer to wrestling prayer, a tangible reality of some kind, that can be seen and handled; a sort of spiritual commodity, done up, as it were, in packages, and labeled "faith," to be stowed away in the heart, ready for use, as a species of coin with which to buy God's gifts, or an equivalent to induce Him to part with them.

In all sorts of ways the subject of faith is often so mixed up with mystery, that a plain, commonsense wayfaring man can make neither head nor tail of the matter in his everyday life. But the truth is that faith is simply neither more nor less than trust or confidence. We have faith in ourselves when we trust ourselves; we have faith in a friend when we trust that friend; we have faith in a bank when we trust that bank. Faith in the Bible sense, therefore, is simply trust or confidence in God. Faith in man and faith in God are precisely the same thing in their nature; the difference consisting only in the different persons believed in. Faith in man links us on to and makes us one with mere humanity; faith in God links us on to and makes us one with divinity.

> If we receive the witness of men, the witness of God is greater: for this is the witness of God which he hath testified of his Son. He that believeth on the Son of God hath the witness in himself: he that believeth not God hath made him a liar; because he believeth not the record that God gave of his Son (1 John 5:9, 10).

Faith, then, is not a thing to be seen, or touched, or handled. It is not a grace, nor a gracious disposition. It is nothing mysterious or perplexing. It is simply and only believing God. And to "exercise faith," as it is called, one has only to exercise towards God the same believing faculty one exercises towards man.

Neither are there different kinds of faith. Men talk about a feeling faith, and a living faith, and a saving faith, and an intellectual faith, and a historical faith, and a dead faith. But it is all a waste of words; for either I trust or I do not trust. If I trust, I have faith, and if I do not trust, I do not have faith, and that is all there is about it.

There are two Scripture illustrations that seem to me to make it very plain what faith really is.

> Through faith we understand that the worlds were framed by the word of God, so that things which are seen were not made of things which do appear (Hebrews 11:3).
>
> (As it is written, I have made thee a father of many nations,) before him whom he believed, even God, who quickeneth the dead, and calleth those things which be not as though they were. Who against hope believed in hope, that he might become the father of many nations, according to that which was spoken, So shall thy seed be. And being not weak in faith, he considered not his own body now dead, when he was about an hundred years old, neither yet the deadness of Sara's womb: He staggered not at the promise of God through unbelief; but was strong in faith, giving glory to God; and being fully persuaded that, what he had promised, he was able also to perform. And therefore it was imputed to him for righteousness (Romans 4:17–22).

The passage in Hebrews simply means that we know that the worlds were framed by the word of God, because God says they were; and we believe Him, without requiring any other proof but His word. We were not there to see them so made, we do not know anybody who was; but God says it, and we believe Him; and this is faith.

The passage in Romans is similar, only that it illustrates faith in regard to a future thing instead of a past thing. Abraham is the Scripture pattern of faith, continually pointed to as such all through the Bible. Now what did Abraham do? He simply believed God, when He told him He was going to give him a son. He had no outward proof of it, and no rational human hope, but "against hope, he believed in hope," because God had said it, and he chose to believe God. And therefore, it is said of him, "Abraham believed God, and it was counted unto him for righteousness."

The "law of faith" appears, therefore, to consist simply in two things, namely, a conviction of God's will, and a perfect confidence that that Will must necessarily be accomplished. There are two passages that seem to me to set forth very clearly and definitely the working of this law.

> And this is the confidence that we have in him, that, if we ask any thing according to his will, he heareth us: And if we know that he hear us, whatsoever we ask, we know that we have the petitions that we desired of him (1 John 5:14, 15).

> And Jesus answering saith unto them, Have faith in God. For verily I say unto you, That whosoever shall say unto this mountain, Be thou removed, and be thou cast into the sea; and shall not doubt in his heart, but shall believe that those things which he saith shall come to pass; he shall have whatsoever he saith. Therefore I say unto you, What things soever ye desire, when ye pray, believe that ye receive them, and ye shall have them (Mark 11:22–24).

Notice the process of faith, or in other words, the "law of faith," as set forth in these passages. We are commanded to have the same sort of faith that God has. (Mark 11:22.) Now God's faith that what He desires will be accomplished, is of course absolute and unwavering. He knows it. And we are to know it also. Then we are to say so.

> For he spake, and it was done; he commanded, and it stood fast (Psalms 33:9).

One passage says "ask," and the other says "say." I believe they are interchangeable words in this connection, and that the prayer of faith is really a command of faith also. "God spake and it was done," and so are we also, who are begotten of Him, to speak, and it shall be done also. This is what it means when it says, "Have the faith of God," as the margin puts it. We are to have the same sort of faith that God has, according to our measure. Romans 4:17 describes the sort of faith God has.

> God, who quickeneth the dead, and calleth those things which be not as though they were.

God disregards all seemings, but, calling "those things which be not as though they were," He creates them by that very calling. How much of this creative power of faith we His children share, I am not prepared to say, but that we are called to share far more of it than we have ever yet laid hold of, I feel very sure. There are, I am convinced, many "mountains" in our lives and experiences, which might be overcome, had we only the courage of faith to say to them, "Be thou removed," accompanied with a calm assurance that they must surely go.

The difficulty is that we neither "say" the word of faith, nor "pray" the prayer of faith. We say generally the word of doubt, and pray the prayer of experiment, and then we wonder why our faith and our prayers are so ineffectual.

> But let him ask in faith, nothing wavering. For he that wavereth is like a wave of the sea, driven with the wind and tossed. For let not that man think that he shall receive any thing of the Lord (James 1:6, 7).

It is of no use to fight against this inevitable law. As well might the architect try to work in opposition to the law of gravitation, and undertake to build his house from the top downwards, as for the Christians to try to accomplish anything in the spiritual realm by means of doubt. It simply cannot be done; and the sooner Christians know this the better for them. How much can be done by faith, may remain an open question perhaps, but it is a settled matter forever that nothing can be done by doubt.

> But without faith it is impossible to please him: for he that cometh to God must believe that he is, and that he is a rewarder of them that diligently seek him (Hebrews 11:6).

Faith is, I believe, the vital principle of the spiritual life, just as truly as breath seems to be the vital principle of the bodily life; and we can no more live spiritually without faith than we can live our bodily life without breath.

As to the limits of the power of faith, I am not, as I said above, prepared to speak. The Scriptures, it seems to me, put no limit whatever. Read the triumphant declaration concerning it in the eleventh chapter of Hebrews. There is scarcely any experience of human life that is not enumerated in one way or another in this magnificent record of faith's achievements and faith's victories.

> And what shall I more say? for the time would fail me to tell of Gedeon, and of Barak, and of Samson, and of Jephthae; of David also, and Samuel, and of the prophets: Who through faith subdued kingdoms, wrought righteousness, obtained promises, stopped the mouths of lions, Quenched the violence of fire, escaped the edge of the sword, out of weakness were made strong, waxed valiant in fight, turned to flight the armies of the aliens. Women received their dead raised to life again: and others were tortured, not accepting deliverance; that they might obtain a better resurrection: and others had trial of cruel mock-

ings and scourgings, yea, moreover, of bonds and imprisonment: They were stoned, they were sawn asunder, were tempted, were slain with the sword: they wandered about in sheepskins and goatskins; being destitute, afflicted, tormented; (Of whom the world was not worthy:) they wandered in deserts, and in mountains, and in dens and caves of the earth. And these all, having obtained a good report through faith, received not the promise: God having provided some better thing for us, that they without us should not be made perfect (Hebrews 11:32–40).

These old worthies surely must have understood the "law of faith," and must have known how to apply it, far better than we do of the present day.

To them this "law" was a law that applied, not only to their religion, but to their life. They brought it into use, not only on fast days or feast days, but on ordinary weekdays as well. They applied it to every emergency. We of the present day make the mistake of limiting the working of this law to what we call the religious part of our life. And yet it is evident that the Bible, in teaching us to "live by faith," must mean our daily living. We are to bring faith to bear upon all that concerns us, whether it is what we call spiritual or what we call temporal; and, in the earthly plane of things, as well as in the heavenly, we are to "overcome by faith." Let us make up our minds, then, to live by the "law of faith." Let us bring it to bear on our household affairs, on our business enterprises, on our social duties, on all and everything, in short, that concerns us, whether it be inward or outward; and see whether we, too, may not "obtain a good report through faith," and may not triumph, as these old worthies did, over every emergency and every need of our lives.

The Law of Life

FOUNDATION TEXT:—For the law of the Spirit of life in Christ Jesus hath made me free from the law of sin and death.—Romans 8:2.

For the most part Christians live their spiritual lives in a very uncertain haphazard sort of way. They are all right on Sundays perhaps, or where the doctrines or services of their religion are concerned, but when it comes to their weekday living they are all at sea. They have no understanding of the "law of life" in its application to this commonplace side of their existence.

In my last lesson on the "law of faith" I tried to put the emphasis on the word *law,* and to show that there is an actual definite "law of faith," which works with the same irresistible certainty as the law of gravitation, or any other natural law. In the same way I desire now to treat the subject of life, emphasizing again the word *law.*

Is it not reasonable to suppose that there must be laws of the spiritual life just as there are laws of the natural life, and that the one must be as sure and dependable in their working as the others? Too often the Christian life is only a series of rather doubtful experiments, whose results are hoped for, but can never be depended upon with any sort of certainty. There seems to be but little conception in most minds that there is an ascertainable and dependable law of life, which, if discovered and understood, would remove our experience out of the region of doubtful chances into the region of assured certainties.

> Thou hast made known to me the ways of life; thou shalt make me full of joy with thy countenance (Acts 2:28).

The only way in which we can be made free from the "law of sin and death," is by the unlimited action of the law of life; and therefore it is of vital importance that we should have made known to us the "ways of life." That is, we must try and discover the "ways" in which spiritual life works, how it is begotten, how it grows, how it is nourished, how it bears fruit, what is its power, and what ought to be its environment.

First, then, let us consider how it is begotten:

> Blessed be the God and Father of our Lord Jesus Christ, which according to his abundant mercy hath begotten us again unto a lively hope by the resurrection of Jesus Christ from the dead (1 Peter 1:3).
> Of his own will begat he us with the word of truth, that we should be a kind of firstfruits of his creatures (James 1:18).
> Which were born, not of blood, nor of the will of the flesh, nor of the will of man, but of God (John 1:13).

Nothing could be more plainly stated. Our spiritual life is begotten of God, of "His own will." Therefore it has its source in Him, and derives its nature from Him. I am convinced very few of us realize this as a fact, else why is it that we struggle so hard to beget a spiritual life in ourselves by our own self efforts? We act often as if we were to be born "of the will of man," and try, by wrestlings, and agonizings, and resolutions, and prayers, and religious "exercises" of all sorts, to bring about the "new birth." No wonder religion has become such a hard and apparently hopeless task to so many. Even on the natural plane, the creation of life is a blank impossibility, and how much more on the spiritual plane. The soul, therefore, that tries by its own self efforts to create spiritual life in itself, is attempting an impossible task, and can land itself nowhere but in despair.

> Jesus answered, Verily, verily, I say unto thee, Except a man be born of water, and of the Spirit, he cannot enter into the kingdom of God. That which is born of the flesh is flesh; and that which is born of the Spirit is spirit. Marvel not that I said unto thee, Ye must be born again. The wind bloweth where it listeth, and thou hearest the sound thereof, but canst not tell whence it cometh, and whither it goeth: so is every one that is born of the Spirit (John 3:5-8).

John alone, of all the Evangelists, records the sayings of our Lord, introduced by the words, "Verily, verily." (There are twenty-four of these sayings in his Gospel, and they all of them develop the laws of the spiritual life.) This "verily, verily," states the incontrovertible fact, that the only way into any form of life is to be born into it. Things grow in a life, but they cannot grow into it. The doorway into any plane of life is always by birth.

> Being born again, not of corruptible seed, but of incorruptible, by the word of God, which liveth and abideth for ever (1 Peter 1:23).
> For verily he took not on him the nature of angels; but he took on him the seed of Abraham. Wherefore in all things it behoved him to be made like unto his brethren, that he might be a merciful and faithful high priest in things pertaining to God, to make reconciliation for the sins of the people (Hebrews 2:16, 17).

In thus taking upon Him the "seed of Abraham," Christ linked Himself on to all humanity for ever. Consequently no human being can be born unlinked to Christ. He was the "first begotten," and in Him, as Head, all humanity has been begotten also.

> For since by man came death, by man came also the resurrection of the dead. For as in Adam all die, even so in Christ shall all be made alive (1 Corinthians 15:21, 22).
> Howbeit that was not first which is spiritual, but that which is natural; and afterward that which is spiritual. The first man is of the earth, earthy: the second man is the Lord from heaven. As is the earthy, such are they also that are earthy: and as is the heavenly, such are they also that are heavenly. And as we have borne the image of the earthy, we shall also bear the image of the heavenly (1 Corinthians 15:46–49).

Clement says somewhere that if we understood the two Adams we should know all truth. Notice the "as" and "so" in 1 Corinthians 15:22. Just as we inherit natural life from the first Adam, so do we inherit spiritual life from the second Adam. There is, therefore, in every man a seed of the divine life, a Christ-germ as it were. The old Quakers called it "the witness of God in the soul," "that which responds to the divine inspeaking."

We may appeal in the case of every man, therefore, to that within which witnesses for God. And thus we shall make the new birth, not a barrier, as is too often done, but a wide and open gateway.

There is a divine seed in every man, but it is not quickened in all. In the natural world seeds may lie dormant, and apparently dead for many years, and yet, when the right conditions are secured, these very seeds will be quickened into a vigorous life.

At a late conference in England I heard Canon Wilberforce describe the quickening of a seed that had been wrapped up in a mummy for thousands of years. It was placed in a little warm water, and he watched it through a microscope. In a few minutes the seed began to swell, then it burst, and little white filaments shot out on every side, waving through the water in search of their proper nourishment. The seed was quickened, and began at once to "lay hold" of life.

> Fight the good fight of faith, lay hold on eternal life, whereunto thou art also called, and hast professed a good profession before many witnesses (1 Timothy 6:12).
> And so it is written, The first man Adam was made a living soul; the last Adam was made a quickening spirit (1 Corinthians 15:45).
> But God, who is rich in mercy, for his great love wherewith he loved us, even when we were dead in sins, hath quickened us together with Christ; by grace ye are saved (Ephesians 2:4, 5).

The divine seed within us is being quickened by the Holy Spirit, whenever we feel inward stirrings and longings after holiness. This is the begetting of God. And then comes in our responsibility. We cannot create life, but we can let life live. We can "lay hold" of it by an entire surrender to Christ, who is our life. We can accept Him as our life, and can refuse to let any other life live in us. We can reckon ourselves to be alive in Him.

> Likewise reckon ye also yourselves to be dead indeed unto sin, but alive unto God through Jesus Christ our Lord (Romans 6:11).

This, then, is how the spiritual life is to grow; that is, by surrender and faith. We must "boycott" the old self-life, and must deal only with the spiritual life. But we must not make another mistake, and think that although we cannot beget life by our self efforts, we are to make it grow ourselves. We are as powerless in the matter of our growth as in the matter of our begetting. Life grows of itself. It is a mighty dynamic force that only asks a chance to grow.

> Which of you by taking thought can add one cubit unto his stature? And why take ye thought for raiment? Consider the lilies of the field

how they grow; they toil not, neither do they spin: And yet I say unto you, That even Solomon in all his glory was not arrayed like one of these. Wherefore, if God so clothe the grass of the field, which today is, and tomorrow is cast into the oven, shall he not much more clothe you, O ye of little faith? (Matthew 6:27–30.)

The lily grows by the power of its inward life principle, and according to the laws of a lily's life. No amount of its own stretching or straining, nor any pulling up by others, would help its growth. It is all folly, and worse than folly, for Christians to make such mighty efforts to grow. If they would only let the Christ life within them grow, unhindered by their interference, they need have no fear of the result. But we are so ignorant of the laws of our spiritual life, that we are continually tempted to meddle with it.

Let us imagine a seed that has just been quickened, communing with itself. "What dreadful place is this I am in? How can anything grow all in the dark like this, and with such heaps of heavy earth on top of it? And, oh dear! what is the matter with me? I seem to be all splitting up! And look at that bit of me going down! I thought I was meant to grow upwards. What does it all mean? I am afraid things are all wrong. And now, just when I thought I was getting out into the nice sunshine, here comes a dreadful storm and drenches me. I never can live through all this. Besides, look how little I am, and I know I was meant to be a big tree. And where is the fruit I was to bear? I have only got two or three tiny green leaves." And so on, and so on, *ad infinitum.*

Have you never known any souls that made similar complaints?

Next we must consider the food of this spiritual life. What are the laws of its nourishment?

Jesus answered them and said, Verily, verily, I say unto you, Ye seek me, not because ye saw the miracles, but because ye did eat of the loaves, and were filled. Labour not for the meat which perisheth, but for that meat which endureth unto everlasting life, which the Son of man shall give unto you: for him hath God the Father sealed. . . . For the bread of God is he which cometh down from heaven, and giveth life unto the world. Then said they unto him, Lord, evermore give us this bread. And Jesus said unto them, I am the bread of life: he that cometh to me shall never hunger; and he that believeth on me shall never thirst (John 6:26, 27, 33–35; see also John 6:48–58).

Christians are continually trying to feed their spiritual life with all sorts of things other than Christ. They feed on the dry husks of dogmas and doctrines, or on forms and ceremonies, or on religious duties well performed, or on Christian work of various kinds, or on good resolutions, or on fervent emotions; and then they wonder at their starved condition. Nothing can really satisfy the hunger of the soul but Christ. He alone can be to the soul all that the soul needs. To draw our life from Christ means to be so united to Him in oneness of nature as that the same spiritual life flows through our spiritual veins as flowed through His. This is a subject I know which is often regarded as very mystical and difficult to understand. I have no intention of dealing with any mystical meanings, but there is a practical commonsense way of looking at the matter, that seems to me simple and easy to understand. We feed ourselves on the writings of a great author by becoming familiar with them, and by adopting their teachings as our own; and in the same way we must feed on Christ. We know what it is to become one in thought and feeling with a beloved and honored friend, and to share that friend's inmost life; and similarly must we become one with Christ. We can understand how an artist can feed his mind on the life and work and teaching of some great master in art, and so become like him, and able, after his measure, to follow in that master's footsteps, and work as he worked; and just so must we do with Christ.*

Next comes the law of life as regards fruit bearing. A living plant always bears fruit. It is the law of its life that it should do so; and it is equally a law that this fruit should come, not by effort, but by spontaneous growth.

> Ye have not chosen me, but I have chosen you, and ordained you, that ye should go and bring forth fruit, and that your fruit should remain: that whatsoever ye shall ask of the Father in my name, he may give it you (John 15:16).

We need not trouble ourselves about our fruit bearing. It is "ordained" that we shall bring it forth, just as it is ordained that a fig tree shall bear figs. It is the law of our spiritual life; and we can no more have real spiritual life within us without bearing fruit than the

---

* See lesson on Soul Food, chapter 2.

oak tree can have life without bearing acorns. Very few seem to understand this; and as a consequence there is a vast amount of effort among Christians to hang fruit on to their branches by some outside performances of one sort or another. It is as if a man should buy apples and hang them on his apple trees, and think thus to secure to himself a good crop of fruit! Fruit must be "brought forth," not fastened on. This is the law of fruit bearing, and to try to violate this law can only bring confusion and death.

> Even so every good tree bringeth forth good fruit; but a corrupt tree bringeth forth evil fruit. A good tree cannot bring forth evil fruit, neither can a corrupt tree bring forth good fruit (Matthew 7:17, 18).

The law of fruit bearing is clearly this, that our fruit can only be the outcome of what we are. Therefore the thing for me to be concerned about is not so much whether my fruit is good or evil, but whether I myself as to my essential self am good or evil.

> Ye shall know them by their fruits. Do men gather grapes of thorns, or figs of thistles? (Matthew 7:16).
> Can the fig tree, my brethren, bear olive berries? either a vine, figs? so can no fountain both yield salt water and fresh (James 3:12).

Another one of the laws of life is that all plants must yield fruit after their own kind. I must be content, therefore, to be just the species of plant, and to bear just the kind of fruit the Divine Husbandman pleases. We do not always find that we invariably like to be what God has made us to be. Perhaps I would like to be a rose bush, and blossom out in roses, when He has made me a potato plant, and wants me to yield potatoes. I might be tempted, in such a case, to get paper roses and sew them on. But what folly! A million paper roses could not turn my potato plant into a rose bush, and the first person who tried to pick one would find me out! All I have to do is to see to it that, of whatever species of plant I may be, whether a homely potato plant or a gorgeous rose, I become a healthy vigorous plant, and fulfill without grumbling the law of my being. Be content to be what thy God has made thee, but do not be content until thou art the best of its kind.

> Abide in me, and I in you. As the branch cannot bear fruit of itself, except it abide in the vine; no more can ye, except ye abide in me (John 15:4).

> Blessed is the man that trusteth in the Lord, and whose hope the Lord is. For he shall be as a tree planted by the waters, and that spreadeth out her roots by the river, and shall not see when heat cometh, but her leaf shall be green; and shall not be careful in the year of drought, neither shall cease from yielding fruit (Jeremiah 17:7, 8).

"Abiding," or in other words, faith, is the law of fruit bearing, as well as of everything else in the spiritual life. If we "abide in Christ," that is, if we live a life of trust in the Lord, we shall not "cease from yielding fruit"; and that fruit will not fail to be good.

Next we must consider what is the law of strength in the spiritual life.

> And he said unto me, My grace is sufficient for thee: for my strength is made perfect in weakness. Most gladly therefore will I rather glory in my infirmities, that the power of Christ may rest upon me (2 Corinthians 12:9).

The law of the spiritual life is that divine strength shall be made perfect in human weakness. Our part is to supply the weakness, God's part is to supply the strength. We are, however, continually trying to usurp God's part and to supply the strength ourselves; and, because we cannot do this, we are plunged into depths of discouragement. We think, in order to work effectively for the Lord, we ought to feel strong in ourselves, and when instead we find ourselves feeling weak, we are in despair. But the Bible teaches us that, if we only knew it, our weakness is in reality our greatest strength.

> And I was with you in weakness, and in fear, and in much trembling. And my speech and my preaching was not with enticing words of man's wisdom, but in demonstration of the Spirit and of power: That your faith should not stand in the wisdom of men, but in the power of God (1 Corinthians 2:3–5).
> But we have this treasure in earthen vessels, that the excellency of the power may be of God, and not of us (2 Corinthians 4:7).

It is of vital importance to the children of God that they should understand the law that God's strength can be made perfect only in human weakness. For in the spiritual life the natural man never can feel strong in itself, and if we think it ought to, we shall be continually troubled. Understanding the law, however, we shall learn, like Paul, to "take pleasure" in our infirmities and our weaknesses, because we shall see that only when we are weak are we really spiritually strong.

> Therefore I take pleasure in infirmities, in reproaches, in necessities, in persecutions, in distresses for Christ's sake: for when I am weak, then am I strong (2 Corinthians 12:10).

The choice lies between the strength of our own human nature, and the strength of the divine nature within us; and we may well be glad to lose the one in order to gain the other. It is like the difference there would be between the power of a seed without life to push up and away the clods above it, and the power of the life in that seed, when it is quickened. To the tiny unquickened mustard seed the weight of earth above it could not but seem like an immovable mountain; but, when quickened, the life within that same tiny seed pushes aside those mountains of earth without any apparent effort. Life carries all before it, and no obstacles can withstand its progress. Even rocks are upheaved by the irresistible power of life in a tiny creeper. It is life, more life that we want, not more effort.

> I am come that they might have life, and that they might have it more abundantly (John 10:10).

The environment of this spiritual life is also subject to a definite law. Every plant has its own laws of life, and can only flourish in certain localities and under certain conditions of soil and climate. And on a higher plane this is equally true of the spiritual life. Outward localities and outward climate make no difference here, although Christians often seem to think they do. We find ourselves in uncongenial surroundings, and are tempted to think our spiritual life cannot flourish in such environments. But no outward circumstances can affect the life of the soul. Its true environment is all inward and spiritual; and this environment is none other than God and His love. "For ye are dead, and your life is hid with Christ in God." This may sound mystical, but it is also the profoundest common sense. The sources of one's life, that is, the objects and aims and underlying springs of action, must be either in self or in God. If in self, then our life is hid in self; if in God, then our life is hid in God; and to "dwell in God," or, in other words, to "abide in Christ," means simply that we have the underlying spring of all our thoughts, words, and actions in Him.

> If a man abide not in me, he is cast forth as a branch, and is withered;
> and men gather them, and cast them into the fire, and they are burned
> (John 15:6).

The reason of so many "withered" lives is to be found in the fact
that they do not "abide in Christ." This is an inevitable law. If a
branch does not abide in the vine it must necessarily wither. The
only environment in which it is possible for the spiritual life to flourish is to "abide in God." And to abide in God means simply to
maintain an unfaltering trust in Him, and a simple obedience to His
will. "If ye keep my commandments you shall abide in my love" is
an unalterable law.

> And we have known and believed the love that God hath to us. God
> is love; and he that dwelleth in love dwelleth in God, and God in him (1
> John 4:16).
> And he that keepeth his commandments dwelleth in him, and he in
> him. And hereby we know that he abideth in us, by the Spirit which he
> hath given us (1 John 3:24).

The man who discovers the law of anything possesses a power in
regard to that thing as limitless as the law itself. And the soul that has
come to a knowledge of the "law of the spirit of life in Christ Jesus"
is truly, as the Apostle says, "made free from the law of sin and
death."

> He that hath an ear, let him hear what the Spirit saith unto the
> churches: To him that overcometh will I give to eat of the tree of life,
> which is in the midst of the paradise of God (Revelation 2:7).
> Thou wilt shew me the path of life: in thy presence is fulness of joy;
> at thy right hand there are pleasures for evermore (Psalms 16:11).

If we will only "hear what the Spirit saith to the churches" on this
subject, He will give us "to eat of the tree of life"; and will reveal to
our spiritual insight that "path of life" in which, if we will faithfully
walk therein, we shall be among those "overcomers" who have come
over or been made free from "the law of sin and death."
It may be asked, however, how we are practically to "eat of the
tree of life"? An illustration may help us here. Let us suppose a person who is dead to the delights of astronomy; who knows nothing
about it, and has no life in the study of it. How is such a person to
become alive to this branch of knowledge? There is only one way,

and that is by studying the subject, by learning its laws, and by obeying them. Such a study may seem very lifeless at first, but, if it is persisted in, sooner or later the mind would become alive to its delights. The student would begin to "eat of the tree of life," and to walk in the "path of life," in regard to astronomy, and would no longer be dead to its charms. In the same way, if we would eat of that tree of life which is in the midst of the paradise of God, we must learn the laws of this life, and must faithfully obey them; and then, sooner or later, we shall be shown the "path of life," and shall triumphantly walk therein.

The Law of Love

FOUNDATION TEXT:—Owe no man any thing, but to love one another: for he that loveth another hath fulfilled the law. For this, Thou shalt not commit adultery, Thou shalt not kill, Thou shalt not steal, Thou shalt not bear false witness, Thou shalt not covet; and if there be any other commandment, it is briefly comprehended in this saying, namely, Thou shalt love thy neighbour as thyself.—Romans 13:8, 9.

In our last two lessons we have considered the law of faith, and the law of life, with an especial emphasis on the word *law*. In this lesson we will take up the law of love, and consider it in a similar manner. That is, we will try to get at the law of love's working, the essence or nature of love, as it were; its inherent and inevitable processes. Love is, I believe, as much a law as gravitation, and, if only we understand the way of its working, may be reckoned on as certainly as gravitation to produce its desired results.

The first law we would notice is that it is in itself the fulfilling of all other laws. "If there be any other commandment," Paul says, after enumerating some of the principal commandments given from Sinai, "if there be any other, it is briefly comprehended in this saying, namely, Thou shalt love thy neighbour as thyself." All laws, therefore, are included and fulfilled in the law of love; and it is, consequently, of the utmost importance to every one of us to discover what this supreme and all-inclusive law is.

For all the law is fulfilled in one word, even in this: Thou shalt love thy neighbour as thyself (Galatians 5:14).

Love worketh no ill to his neighbour; therefore love is the fulfilling of the law (Romans 13:10).

140

The most essential law of love is here stated, that characteristic of it which makes it inclusive of all other laws, namely, "Love worketh no ill to his neighbor." It is the very nature of love that it cannot by any possibility work ill to its neighbor, knowing it to be ill. It is as impossible as it would be for the sun to give darkness instead of light. Love loves, and cannot therefore do anything contrary to love. It is not that it will not or ought not, but simply and only that it CANNOT. It is an absolutely inevitable law.

We must remember, however, that a great deal of what is called love ought really to be spelled s-e-l-f-i-s-h-n-e-s-s. People love their own enjoyment of their friends more than they love the friends themselves, and consider their own welfare in their intercourse with those they profess to love, far more than the welfare of the so-called loved ones. It has been said that we never really love anyone until we can do without them for their good; and, measured by this test, how few there are who really love. How many lives are marred and made miserable by the selfishness of some relative or friend (too often, alas! a parent), who, under the plea of exceeding love, will not allow the least liberty of action in the loved ones, and will do everything possible to hinder their development in every line that does not conduce to their own personal pleasure, or is not agreeable to themselves. Surely such a course, however it may be disguised, can spring from nothing but pure unadulterated selfishness.

The law of love can never be a cherishing of self at the expense of the loved one, but must always be the cherishing of the loved one at the expense of self.

Let no man seek his own, but every man another's wealth (1 Corinthians 10:24).

In considering the law of love, therefore, we must settle this fact first of all, that real love has no selfishness in it whatever. It never "seeks its own" good, but the good of the loved one. It forgets self; or, in other words, it reckons self to have no claims, and no rights, except the right to love, and to spend itself on those it loves. This is the way a true mother loves, with a self-forgetfulness that leads her to lay down her very life itself, if need be, for her children. This is the way Christ loved us while we were yet sinners, when He died for us. This is the sort of love the poet meant when he said—

> Love of God, of such great loving
> Only mothers know the cost;
> Cost of love, that, all love passing,
> Gave itself to save the lost.

With this understanding of the "law of love," we will now consider that law in two aspects, namely, as it affects God's relations to us, and as it affects our relations to our fellow men.

And, first, I would say that it is absolutely impossible for us to know God at all, unless we know something of what love is; for "God is love." He is as it were made out of love. Therefore, the Apostle says:—

> Beloved, let us love one another: for love is of God; and every one that loveth is born of God, and knoweth God. He that loveth not knoweth not God; for God is love (1 John 4:7, 8).

God is love; therefore love is the key to the mystery of God. He is not only loving, but He is infinitely more than that; He is love itself. The sun not only gives light, but it is light, the source, and center, and very being of light itself; and this always, although the fact may be hidden from our eyes by clouds, or misrepresented by colored or smoked glass.

We have all used the expression, "God is love," hundreds of times, no doubt; but I am afraid it has conveyed to our minds no more real idea of the facts of the case than if we had said, "God is wood."

If we would know God, therefore, we must know what love is; and then we must apply to God all the best and highest that we know of love. For God is absolutely under the law of love; that is, He is under an inevitable constraint to obey it. He alone of all the universe, because His very essence or nature is love, cannot help loving. We, alas! whose natures are not altogether composed of love, but are mixed up with a great many other things, can help loving, and very often do help it. And because this is the case with ourselves, we think it must also be the case with Him; and we torment ourselves with imagining that, because of our own especial unworthiness, He will surely fail to love us. What a useless torment it is! How little common sense there is in it!

And we have known and believed the love that God hath to us. God is love; and he that dwelleth in love dwelleth in God, and God in him (1 John 4:16).

More than anything else, we need to find out "the love that God hath to us." All difficulties, all anxieties, all fears, all perplexities, disappear when the soul has made this discovery. I say "find out," because the love exists just the same whether we know it or not, but we do not get the comfort of it, though we may get the good, unless we find it out.

This is plain common sense. But I fear a great many people have an idea that they are obliged to create God's love themselves; and they try, therefore, in every possible way to accomplish the impossible feat. This mistake lies at the root of all asceticism and of all legal efforts. We are simply trying by these means to create love toward ourselves in the heart of God; forgetting in our foolishness that all love "is of God," and cannot come from any other source.

For scarcely for a righteous man will one die: yet peradventure for a good man some would even dare to die. But God commendeth his love toward us, in that, while we were yet sinners, Christ died for us (Romans 5:7, 8).

One of the laws of love is that it loves for love's sake only, and not because of anything lovable in the object. How often we have seen mothers lavishing a wealth of love upon children who did not seem to others to possess one single lovable quality. One of my children once said to me, in a fit of remorse after a spell of naughtiness, "Oh, Mother, I do not see how you *can* love such a naughty little girl as I am." And I replied, "Ah, darling, you cannot understand. I do not love you for what you are, but I love you for what I am. I am your mother, and I love you because of my mother-heart of love; and I should love you just the same no matter what you did. I should not love your naughtiness, but I should love you."

The Lord did not set his love upon you, nor choose you, because ye were more in number than any people; for ye were the fewest of all people; But because the Lord loved you, and because he would keep the oath which he had sworn unto your fathers, hath the Lord brought you out with a mighty hand, and redeemed you out of the house of bondmen, from the hand of Pharaoh king of Egypt (Deuteronomy 7:7, 8).

The Lord has not "set His love" upon us because of anything we are, nor because of anything we have done or can do. He has set His love upon us simply and only because it is a law of love to love that which it creates. He cannot help loving us. His love flows out of His own divine heart of love, exactly as a mother's love flows out of her mother-heart upon her little helpless child. It is the "law of love" that it shall love for "love's sake only."

> Unto him that loved us, and washed us from our sins in his own blood (Revelation 1:5).

Notice the order here. He loves first, and then He washes. He did not love us because we were washed, but He washes us because He loves us. This is the law of love.

If a darling child should be stolen from its mother, and carried by tramps into a life of dirt, and misery, and rags, and if that mother should one day discover it by the wayside, ragged and dirty, would she draw back in disgust and say, "Oh, do not ask me to love such a dirty child as that! Let it get washed; and then bring it to me, and I will love it." Ah, dear mothers, we know better than that! We know how we would rush to our child and clasp it in our arms, regardless of its dirt, and take it home to wash it and make it clean; and, although we might take more comfort in it after it was washed, we would not love it one bit better than we did while it was covered with rags and dirt.

> The Lord hath appeared of old unto me, saying, Yea, I have loved thee with an everlasting love: therefore with lovingkindness have I drawn thee (Jeremiah 31:3).

Another law of divine love is, that it is everlasting. It has had no beginning, and can have no end. So little is this understood, that many people have a rooted conviction that God only begins to love them after they have shown Him that they love Him; and that He ceases to love them the moment they in any way displease Him. They look upon His love as a fickle sort of thing, not in the least to be depended upon, and are always questioning whether they may reckon it to be theirs or not.

> Herein is love, not that we loved God, but that he loved us, and sent his Son to be the propitiation for our sins (1 John 4:10).

Hereby perceive we the love of God, because he laid down his life for us: and we ought to lay down our lives for the brethren (1 John 3:16).

There is no fear in love; but perfect love casteth out fear: because fear hath torment. He that feareth is not made perfect in love (1 John 4:18).

Could we but really "perceive the love of God," we should never again know a moment of "fear," let the outlook be as dark or dangerous as it might. There is no fear in love; there cannot be in the very nature of things. Such is the "law of love."

We have in the thirteenth chapter of 1 Corinthians a wonderful exposition of the "law of love."

If we translate the word *charity* here, as it really is in the original, by the word *love,* we shall more clearly understand these laws.

Love suffereth long.

Love is kind.

Love envieth not.

Love vaunteth not itself.

Love is not puffed up.

Love doth not behave itself unseemly.

Love seeketh not her own.

Love is not easily provoked.

Love thinketh no evil.

Love rejoiceth not in iniquity.

Love rejoiceth in the truth.

Love beareth all things.

Love believeth all things.

Love hopeth all things.

Love endureth all things.

Love never faileth.

This sort of love could not be spelled s-e-l-f-i-s-h-n-e-s-s!

Let us apply each one of these laws, then, in two ways: first, to define God's relations to us, and, second, to teach us what ought to be our relations to one another.

A new commandment I give unto you, That ye love one another; as I have loved you, that ye also love one another. By this shall all men know that ye are my disciples, if ye have love one to another (John 13:34, 35).

We all have an ideal as to what love between human beings ought to be, and we realize a sense of condemnation whenever we fail to come up to our standard. Now if it is true that we are to love one another as Christ loves us, the converse must be true also, that Christ must love us as we know we ought to love one another. In other words, the law of love from God to us is exactly the same as the law of love from us to one another; and what love demands from me to my brother or sister, is what love demands from God to me. This is a far more vital point than might appear at first, for wrong views of the love of God lie, I am convinced, at the root of most of our spiritual difficulties. We take the worst elements in our own characters, our selfishness, our impatience, our suspiciousness, our hard thoughts of one another, as the key to interpret God, instead of taking our best elements, of love, and self-sacrifice, and patience, as the key. And so we subverse every single law of love in our interpretation of God, who is love itself.

It is one of the laws of love that it suffereth long and is kind. Some of us understand this law in human relations, and will suffer and be kind toward our loved ones all our lives long. But when it comes to God, we think that, although we ought to suffer long, He cannot, and that He very easily gets impatient with our waywardness and our sin. As if such a thing were possible of God who is love!

Another law of love is, that it vaunteth not itself, and seeketh not its own; and wherever we see these elements manifested, we say of such so-called love that it is not really love at love, but only and wholly selfishness. And yet, by the strange perversion of things that seem to have somehow crept into our ideas of God, we think it all right to look upon Him as always seeking to vaunt Himself, and as being continually on the lookout for His own glory. We seem to think that self-seeking, which is so hateful in ourselves, is somehow all right in Him; forgetting that the "law of love" must be the same both for ourselves and for Him, and that what would be contrary to this law in us, would also be contrary to it in Him.

Still another law of love is, that it is not easily provoked, and that it thinks no evil, but beareth all things, believeth all things, hopeth all things, and endureth all things. We mothers understand this law, and are always thinking the best of our children, believing, and hoping, and enduring, until the end of our lives. If the child is naughty, we say, "Poor darling, she is sick"; or, "Poor boy, we must remember his temptations." But the same mother perhaps will think of God as if He were always looking out with an unfriendly eye for the least imperfection in herself, and were even putting the worst possible construction upon her motives, thinking evil of her even when she has really meant all right.

Another law of love is, that it never faileth. All other things are unstable, and are liable to fail at the critical moment; but love never. Nothing baffles it, nothing wears it out, nothing overcomes it. It is all-conquering and all-embracing.

> Many waters cannot quench love, neither can the floods drown it: if a man would give all the substance of his house for love, it would utterly be contemned (Song of Solomon 8:7).

We know that sometimes the love of poor human mothers is of this unquenchable sort, but have we ever really believed the love of God was? Could anything trouble us, if we did so believe?

Ah, dear friends, if we only knew it, the love of God is sweeping toward us in an all-victorious, unfailing flood of mighty tenderness, that is achieving for each one of His children magnificent results, whether they know it or not. It is one of the laws of love that it is absolutely compelled to do the very best it can for its loved ones. God then, because He is love, must be at this very moment doing the very best He can for each one of us, and must always have been doing so, and must always continue to do so. He is absolutely compelled to do it, because He is love. Things may look as hard or as disastrous as they please, but we, who know something of the "law of love," KNOW that all things are working together for our good, and are all ordered by tenderest love.

> Who shall separate us from the love of Christ? shall tribulation, or distress, or persecution, or famine, or nakedness, or peril, or sword? As it is written, For thy sake we are killed all the day long; we are accounted as sheep for the slaughter. Nay, in all these things we are more than conquerors through him that loved us. For I am persuaded that neither death, nor life, nor angels, nor principalities, nor powers, nor things present, nor things to come, Nor height, nor depth, nor any other creature, shall be able to separate us from the love of God, which is in Christ Jesus our Lord (Romans 8:35–39).

Oh! let us be certain about God's love for us! I know that we are poor, weak, failing creatures, and that often we are so disgusted with ourselves as to feel as if God also must be disgusted with us. But we must not let in such thoughts. That is not the way of love in mothers, nor the way of love in God either. "Nothing can separate" love from its object. It is one of the laws of love that instead of being driven away, it is drawn closer by the needs of its loved ones. It takes their sins and sorrows upon itself, and cannot help doing so.

> In all their affliction he was afflicted, and the angel of his presence saved them: in his love and in his pity he redeemed them; and he bare them, and carried them all the days of old (Isaiah 63:9).

What a motherly God is here revealed to us! Have we ever half appreciated Him?

Having thus seen what the "law of love" is as it affects God's relations to us, let us now consider it in its application to our relations with one another.

> Be ye therefore followers of God, as dear children; And walk in love, as Christ also hath loved us, and hath given himself for us an offering and a sacrifice to God for a sweet smelling savour (Ephesians 5:1, 2; see also John 15:12; 1 John 4:11, 12).

All we have said about the law of love applies here. We must "walk in love as Christ hath loved us." That *as* is a word of tremendous import. Do we know anything of its meaning experimentally?

> He that saith he is in the light, and hateth his brother, is in darkness even until now. He that loveth his brother abideth in the light, and there is none occasion of stumbling in him. But he that hateth his brother is in darkness, and walketh in darkness, and knoweth not whither he goeth, because that darkness hath blinded his eyes (1 John 2:9, 11; see also 1 John 3:10–15).

Let us turn back to the sixteen laws of love given to us in 1 Corinthians 13:4–8, and test our love for one another by them. For it is very evident that this love is an exceedingly vital matter in our soul-life. "He that loveth not his brother abideth in death." Tested by the laws of love that we have been considering, who of us can say that he really loves?

All other gifts or graces are valueless in the sight of God, if this one grace of love is wanting. "Though I speak with the tongue of men and angels and have not love, I am become as a sounding brass or a tinkling cymbal." What becomes then of all the fine sermons preached from unloving hearts, or the eloquent discourses uttered by bitter lips?

But there is more than this. "Though I have the gift of prophecy, and understand all mysteries, and all knowledge; and though I have all faith, so that I could remove mountains, and have not love, I am nothing." Then what about the stern sectarian whose zeal for the Cause (with a capital C) leads him into such unloving words and actions?

But there is still even more. "Though I bestow all my goods to feed the poor, and though I give my body to be burned, and have not love, it profiteth me nothing." What then are we to think of a large part of the charities and so-called martyrdoms of Christians nowadays, whose hearts seem set rather on judging than on loving one another?

It is of no use to shirk the question, dear reader. We must love our brethren with this divine, unselfish love, or, in spite of all our gifts, we are nothing but "sounding brass or a tinkling cymbal."

Neither is it our brethren only that we are to love.

> Ye have heard that it hath been said, Thou shalt love thy neighbour, and hate thine enemy. But I say unto you, Love your enemies, bless them that curse you, do good to them that hate you, and pray for them which despitefully use you, and persecute you; That ye may be the children of your Father which is in heaven: for he maketh his sun to rise on the evil and on the good, and sendeth rain on the just and on the unjust. For if ye love them which love you, what reward have ye? do not even the publicans the same? And if ye salute your brethren only, what do ye more than others? do not even the publicans so? Be ye therefore perfect, even as your Father which is in heaven is perfect (Matthew 5:43–48).

The perfection here spoken of is the perfection of love. In order to be the "children of our Father," in the only true sense of this expression, namely, oneness of nature and character, we must love our enemies, for He loves His enemies. This exhortation of our Lord's would of course lose all its point if God did not love His enemies. To my mind no more tremendous assertion of God's universal love to all mankind, even to those who are His enemies, is made throughout the whole Bible than is incidentally contained in this passage. I am to love my enemies because God loves His. If He does not love His enemies, than I need not love mine. It is as clear as daylight.

But this is only by the way. The point of the passage is, that if I would be perfect in my measure, as God is in His, I must love. Love is the sign-manual and the test.

> Beloved, let us love one another: for love is of God; and every one that loveth is born of God, and knoweth God. He that loveth not knoweth not God; for God is love. Beloved, if God so loved us, we ought also to love one another. No man hath seen God at any time. If we love one another, God dwelleth in us, and his love is perfected in us (1 John 4:7, 8, 11, 12).

> In this the children of God are manifest, and the children of the devil: whosoever doeth not righteousness is not of God, neither he that loveth not his brother. For this is the message that ye heard from the beginning, that we should love one another. Not as Cain, who was of that wicked one, and slew his brother. And wherefore slew he him? Because his own works were evil, and his brother's righteous. Marvel not, my brethren, if the world hate you. We know that we have passed from death unto life, because we love the brethren. He that loveth not his brother abideth in death. Whosoever hateth his brother is a murderer: and ye know that no murderer hath eternal life abiding in him. Hereby perceive we the love of God, because he laid down his life for us: and we ought to lay down our lives for the brethren (1 John 3:10–16).

Did we but love after this fashion all victories would be possible to us. Love is as irresistible as dynamite. No barriers can withstand its overcoming power. The cruelest enemy or the hardest sinner must bow before it. I once heard of a woman who was like a wild beast in her brutal ferocity. No one, at the risk of their lives, dared approach her, unless they were armed with a revolver. But a Christian woman, who loved sinners, went into her cell, armed only with words and looks of love, and stooping over her, as she crouched in a corner like a tiger ready to spring, kissed her forehead, and said, "My dear sister." In a moment the fountains of that poor sinner's heart were unsealed, and she poured out floods of tears and sobs of penitent anguish. She was saved by the "law of love."

I seem to get glimpses now and then of what life would be for all of us, if we but knew and lived by this "law of love"; what infinite rest Godward, and what mighty power man-ward would be ours! God grant it speedily!

I say to thee—do thou repeat
  To the first man thou mayest meet
In lane, highway, or open street—

That he, and we, and all men move
  Under a canopy of love,
As broad as the blue sky above;

That doubt and trouble, fear, and pain,
  And anguish, all are shadows vain;
That death itself shall not remain;

That weary deserts we may tread,
  A dreary labyrinth may thread,
Through dark ways underground be led;

Yet if we will our Guide obey,
  The dreariest path, the darkest way
Shall issue out in heavenly day.

And we, on divers shores now cast,
  Shall meet, our perilous voyage past,
All in our Father's house at last.

And ere thou leave him, say thou this
  Yet one word more,—They only miss
The winning of that final bliss,

Who will not count it true, that Love,
  Blessing, not cursing, rules above,
And that in it we live and move.

And one thing farther make him know,—
  That to believe these things are so,
This firm faith never to forego,

Despite of all that seems at strife,
  With blessing, all with curses rife,
That this is blessing, this is life.
                              —R. C. TRENCH

The Law of Righteousness

FOUNDATION TEXT:—What shall we say then? That the Gentiles, which followed not after righteousness, have attained to righteousness, even the righteousness which is of faith. But Israel, which followed after the law of righteousness, hath not attained to the law of righteousness.—Romans 9:30, 31.

We have been considering the laws of many things in the spiritual life, but none are more important for everyday religion than the one we are to consider in this lesson, namely, the law of righteousness. On no subject is there more misunderstanding. Everyone realizes that righteousness is absolutely vital to the spiritual life, not only on Sundays but each day in the week as well; and every child of God "follows after" it with eager quest. But, like the Israelites of whom our text speaks, how many there are who do not attain to it; and whose souls cry out in bitter questioning, "Wherefore?" Let the Scriptures answer their cry.

Wherefore? Because they sought it not by faith, but as it were by the works of the law. For they stumbled at that stumblingstone; As it is written, Behold, I lay in Sion a stumblingstone and rock of offence: and whosoever believeth on him shall not be ashamed (Romans 9:32, 33).

"Because they sought it not by faith." No answer could be clearer than this. Faith is the law of spiritual righteousness, and righteousness is to be attained in no other way. No amount of works, however religious, can bring about true holiness. Outward doings can never take the soul into the inner sanctuary of the righteousness of God.

The reason of this is evident. God's righteousness is a righteousness of nature or being, and outward doings can never create inward life; they can only reveal it. God is not righteous because He does righteous deeds, but He does righteous deeds because He is righteous. This is the essential difference between the righteousness of faith and the righteousness of works. The last is a righteousness put on from the outside, the first springs up from within. The one is works, the other is fruit.

> For I say unto you, That except your righteousness shall exceed the righteousness of the scribes and Pharisees, ye shall in no case enter into the kingdom of heaven (Matthew 5:20).
> Woe unto you, scribes and Pharisees, hypocrites! for ye pay tithe of mint and anise and cummin, and have omitted the weightier matters of the law, judgment, mercy, and faith: these ought ye to have done, and not to leave the other undone. Ye blind guides, which strain at a gnat and swallow a camel. Woe unto you, scribes and Pharisees, hypocrites! for ye make clean the outside of the cup and of the platter, but within they are full of extortion and excess. Thou blind Pharisee, cleanse first that which is within the cup and platter that the outside of them may be clean also. Woe unto you, scribes and Pharisees, hypocrites! for ye are like unto whited sepulchres, which indeed appear beautiful outward, but are within full of dead men's bones, and of all uncleanness. Even so ye also outwardly appear righteous unto men, but within ye are full of hypocrisy and iniquity (Matthew 23:23–28).

No sin in all the Bible receives such utter condemnation as this one of substituting an outward righteousness of doing for an inward righteousness of being. A man may "appear" ever so righteous outwardly, but if his inward springs of life are "full of extortion and excess," there is no real righteousness in anything he does. The law of spiritual righteousness is above all things this, that it is real. And to be real, it must be inward; not inward only of course, but inward first, before it reveals itself outwardly.

> But this shall be the covenant that I will make with the house of Israel; After those days, saith the Lord, I will put my law in their inward parts, and write it in their hearts; and will be their God, and they shall be my people (Jeremiah 31:33).
> For the Lord seeth not as man seeth; for man looketh on the outward appearance, but the Lord looketh on the heart (1 Samuel 16:7).

Even on the earthly plane we recognize that the "outward appearance" is very often no indication of any real thing inside; and we value the kind deeds our friends do for us only in proportion as we believe them to be the manifestation of an inward reality. That which is on the outside only, has no charm, even to human eyes. Much more then can we understand that this must be the case with God.

> Ye hypocrites, well did Esaias prophesy of you, saying, This people draweth nigh unto me with their mouth, and honoureth me with their lips; but their heart is far from me. But in vain they do worship me, teaching for doctrines the commandments of men (Matthew 15:7-9).

It is all "in vain" for us to think that any righteousness which is only outside can be acceptable to God, or of any worth to ourselves. Nothing was more universally condemned by our Lord, and nothing was more despised by the Apostles. If ever any man had that wherein he might glory as to outward righteousness, Paul had. He had been zealous and faithful in all that his religion demanded of him, and could even say of himself that "touching the righteousness that is in the law" he had been blameless; and yet, in the face of the reality of true inward righteousness in Christ, he counted all this outward righteousness to be but dung, that he might "win Christ and be found in Him, not having his own righteousness, which is of the law, but that which is through the faith of Christ, the righteousness which is of God by faith" (*see* Philippians 3:4-9).

Paul had learned that only the "righteousness which is of God by faith" could satisfy the longings of his awakened spiritual nature. And every child of God since must learn the same lesson. Our souls cry out for something that is real. We go through all the faithful round of outward doings; we give up this; we consent to that; we perform every known duty; we are obedient to all requirements; and yet we are not satisfied. We feel, as our Lord Himself has said, that the righteousness that belongs to the kingdom of God must "exceed" this outward righteousness, just as the inward reality always exceeds the outward show; and we cannot be satisfied short of it.

> Brethren, my heart's desire and prayer to God for Israel is, that they might be saved. For I bear them record that they have a zeal of God, but not according to knowledge. For they being ignorant of God's

righteousness, and going about to establish their own righteousness, have not submitted themselves unto the righteousness of God (Romans 10:1–3).

Dear reader, I would appeal to your own experience, and ask whether the case of Israel is not also your own case? Are you not conscious of having a "zeal of God" after righteousness, that has never yet been realized? Do you not feel that your expectations at conversion, as to the righteousness, peace, and joy in the Holy Ghost, which you then understood were to be the characteristics of your new life, have failed to become your portion? Is there not some terrible deficiency in your experience, for which you do not know how to account? The passage quoted above explains all this. You have been trying to establish your own righteousness, and have not known how to submit yourselves to the righteousness of God.

For Christ is the end of the law for righteousness to every one that believeth (Romans 10:4).

Christ is the end of all our self efforts after righteousness; not "at the end," as I used to think, but the actual ending of them. For He is our righteousness. That is, the life of Christ in our souls is a righteous life, which produces all right outward actions by the power of its inward workings; and therefore, in the very nature of things, puts an end to any need for "going about to establish our own righteousness." Instead of our trying to take possession of righteousness, the life of Christ in the soul makes righteousness take possession of us. We are controlled from within, and not from without.

Therefore by the deeds of the law there shall no flesh be justified in his sight: for by the law is the knowledge of sin. But now the righteousness of God without the law is manifested, being witnessed by the law and the prophets; Even the righteousness of God which is by faith of Jesus Christ unto all and upon all them that believe: for there is no difference (Romans 3:20–22).

The law then by which this "righteousness of God" works is the law of faith. You have understood this law as regards the forgiveness of your sins, and learned long ago, perhaps, how you must lay aside all legal efforts to earn or purchase forgiveness for yourselves, and must take it by simple faith as a gift from the Lord Jesus Christ. But when it came to righteousness, this has seemed to you, it may be, a different matter, and you have honestly thought you ought to bring it about by your own self-efforts. You have failed to notice the significance of the "as" and "so" in the verse which says, "As ye have therefore received Christ Jesus the Lord, so walk ye in Him." You received Him by simple faith alone, and you must walk in Him by simple faith alone also. This was the secret Luther discovered on that memorable day in Rome, as he was climbing on his knees up the stairs in the Vatican, hoping to make himself righteous thereby. When he was halfway up he was suddenly arrested by the voice of God sounding in his heart the words, "The just shall live by faith"; and he saw, as in a vision, that the righteousness of God, the only sort of righteousness with which his soul could be satisfied, was to come by faith and by faith alone; and he rose from his knees a new man.

> For whatsoever is born of God overcometh the world: and this is the victory that overcometh the world, even our faith. Who is he that overcometh the world, but he that believeth that Jesus is the Son of God? (1 John 5:4, 5).
> I am crucified with Christ: nevertheless I live; yet not I, but Christ liveth in me: and the life which I now live in the flesh I live by the faith of the Son of God, who loved me, and gave himself for me. I do not frustrate the grace of God: for if righteousness come by the law, then Christ is dead in vain (Galatians 2:20, 21).

Not only were we made alive in the first place by Christ, but moment by moment we must live in Him. When temptations arise we must no longer try to conquer them ourselves; we must not meet them with our own resolves or our own efforts; we must meet them simply with the Lord. We must hide in Him as within the walls of a Gibraltar, and make Him our "strong refuge." In the language of an old writer, we must say to Him, "Lord, thou hast declared that sin shall not have dominion over thy people. I believe this word of thine cannot be broken; and therefore, helpless in myself, I rely upon thy faithfulness to save me from the dominion of the sins which now tempt me. Put forth thy power, O Lord Christ, and get thyself great glory in subduing my flesh, with its affections and lusts." Then, having thus committed our temptations to Him, we must believe that He has undertaken to deliver us, and we must leave ourselves in His care. We must stand by, and let Him fight. And we shall find, to our unutterable rejoicing, that He DOES deliver, according to His word. The enemy flees from His presence, and the soul is enabled to be "more than conqueror" through Him.

This is the law of God's righteousness, under the covenant of grace. The righteousness of the old covenant was not like this. It began at the opposite end. It put works first, and life last, as the result of works; while the new covenant puts life first, and works last, as the result of life. The one said, "This do, and thou shalt live"; the other says, "Live, and then thou shalt do." The old covenant was a law imposed from the outside. The new covenant is a law written within.

> For this is the covenant that I will make with the house of Israel after those days, saith the Lord; I will put my laws into their mind, and write them in their hearts; and I will be to them a God, and they shall be to me a people; And they shall not teach every man his neighbour, and every man his brother, saying, Know the Lord: for all shall know me, from the least to the greatest ... In that he saith, A new covenant, he hath made the first old. Now that which decayeth and waxeth old is ready to vanish away (Hebrews 8:10, 11, 13).

If righteousness could have come under the covenant of works, then "no place would have been sought" for a new covenant. But it could not so come; not, however, because of any arbitrary enactment of God, but because of the very nature of things which makes it inevitable that works must always be the result of life, and never life the result of works. Faith, and faith only, is the divine law of righteousness.

> For Moses describeth the righteousness which is of the law, That the man which doeth those things shall live by them. But the righteousness which is of faith speaketh on this wise, Say not in thine heart, Who shall ascend into heaven? (that is, to bring Christ down from above:) Or, Who shall descend into the deep? (that is, to bring up Christ again from the dead.) But what saith it? The word is nigh thee, even in thy mouth, and in thy heart: that is, the word of faith, which we preach; That if thou shalt confess with thy mouth the Lord Jesus, and shalt believe in thine heart that God hath raised him from the dead, thou shalt be saved. For with the heart man believeth unto righteousness; and with the mouth confession is made unto salvation (Romans 10:5–10).

"The righteousness which is of faith" speaketh to us here in un-mistakable terms. "With the heart man believeth unto righteous-ness." "With the heart," that is with the inner man, the central "ego" of our being. If this inner man takes up an attitude of faith for righ-teousness, righteousness cannot fail to come. This is the law of a righteous life; and it is good plain common sense as well. Out of the heart are the issues of life, and out of nothing else. And the heart, or, in other words, the inner man, works by faith and by faith alone. By faith therefore, we must reckon ourselves dead to sin, and by faith we must reckon ourselves alive unto righteousness. By faith we must put off the old man, and by faith we must put on the new man. We must turn our back on self and all self's activities; and, ceasing from our own works, we must suffer Christ to work in us "to will and to do of His good pleasure."

> But of him are ye in Christ Jesus, who of God is made unto us wis-dom, and righteousness, and sanctification, and redemption (1 Corinthians 1:30).
> Likewise reckon ye also yourselves to be dead indeed unto sin, but alive unto God through Jesus Christ our Lord. Let not sin therefore reign in your mortal body, that ye should obey it in the lusts thereof. Neither yield ye your members as instruments of unrighteousness unto sin: but yield yourselves unto God, as those that are alive from the dead, and your members as instruments of righteousness unto God. For sin shall not have dominion over you: for ye are not under the law, but under grace (Romans 6:11–14).

The inner working of the law of righteousness is revealed here in the two words "reckon" and "yield." These are the things we have to do, God does all the rest. This is the attitude of faith.

I can best illustrate my meaning by the experience of a little girl of my acquaintance. She was a child of about seven years, and was, as her mother believed, a little Christian, with a very simple but real faith in her Saviour. She was, however, sometimes quite naughty. One night as she was going to bed, she said to her mother, "Mother, what can be the reason that I am so naughty? I know I am one of Jesus' lambs, and I thought His lambs were always good; but though I try and try as hard as I can, I am not always good." Her mother, who knew something about the unalterable working of this law of righteousness, said, "The reason is, darling, that you are trying to be good in your own strength, and are not trusting the Lord to make you good."

"Of course I am," the child replied. "That is the only way there is to be good, to just try and try as hard as you can."

"Oh, no," said the mother, "that is not the way at all. You never can be good that way. You must just trust Jesus to make you good."

"I don't believe that at all," said the child indignantly. "I believe the way is to make up your mind to be good, and then to put all your will into it, and just try."

The mother tried to explain the law of righteousness, somewhat as it has been set forth in this lesson, and told the little girl that she herself had tried all ways of being good, and had never succeeded until she trusted the Lord to make and keep her good. But all was in vain. The little girl persisted that she knew she could be good, if she only tried hard enough; and that she was sure that was the way.

Finally, the mother thought of a plan, and said, "Very well, darling, if you will be good for a whole month by your own efforts, I will give you fifty dollars." The child was delighted, and eagerly embraced her mother's offer. "I will begin tomorrow," she cried with eager anticipation, "and I know I shall be good every minute of the time, for I am just going to put my whole will into it, and make myself be good."

The next morning the little girl was awake bright and early, and called out eagerly from her little bed, "Well, Mother, I am going to begin being good today, and you had better write down what day of the month it is, so as to keep a safe account." The mother agreed. Then in a few minutes the child added, as if after a little thought about the difficulties that might beset her, "But mind, Mother, nobody must be provoking." This was promised, and the day began.

In about ten minutes there was not a naughtier little girl in that whole neighborhood; and all that day, and the next, and the next the naughtiness continued. The mother said nothing, thinking it best to wait for the Holy Spirit to teach the child Himself.

At the close of the third day, as the mother was tucking up her darling for the night, the little girl burst out with, "Well, Mother, I am cured at last." "Cured," repeated the mother in surprise, "cured of what?" "Why, cured of trying to make myself good," replied the child. "It is not a bit of use, for I did try just as hard as ever I could, and I could not be good. And besides," she added, "I found out, that even if I could be good outside, it would not be good inside, so where was the use?"

Silently thanking God for His divine teaching, the mother assured the child that, now she had found out her own helplessness, she might with confidence trust the Lord to make her good; and tried to tell her in simple language how to do this. The childish heart seemed to comprehend the "law of righteousness," and joyfully put itself into the hands of the Lord, that He might give the victory.

"Do you tell everybody this, Mother?" she asked earnestly at last. "For I am sure there must be lots of people just like me, who think they can be good in their own strength; and they ought to know." Then, as her mother leaned over the little cot for the last farewell kiss, the child added her final childish prayer, "Dear Lord, I thank Thee for curing me of that foolish notion; and if I am not all cured tonight, please let me be all cured by tomorrow morning. Amen!"

"Sit Still"

FOUNDATION TEXT:—For the Egyptians shall help in vain, and to no purpose: therefore have I cried concerning this, Their strength is to sit still.—Isaiah 30:7.

There is immense power in stillness. All of God's greatest creative works are done in silence. All the vital functions of our bodies are silently performed. The moment they make a noise, we are sure they are out of order. If I can hear the beating of my heart, I know at once that something is wrong. If my brain makes a buzzing noise in my ears, I am afraid that I have brain disease.

This is far more true of spiritual forces. Their work is always done in the stillness. Faith, that mightiest of all spiritual powers, makes no noise in its inward exercise. The new birth is silently accomplished. The Spirit of God works noiselessly within our hearts, and effects all its mighty transformations in deepest stillness. The "creature" in us may accompany all these processes with noise and bustle, but as to the process itself, we must all recognize that it is silently wrought.

This being the case, one would suppose that we could not fail to understand the truth of the declaration that our "strength is to sit still." And perhaps on the Sabbaths of life we do catch some glimmerings of this fact. But our weekdays are so full of bustle and activity that it is difficult for us to see how it can be possible to "sit still" in the midst of it all. We are accustomed, on the plane of matter, to accomplish all our results by active work and struggle, and it is hard for us to understand how it can be different on the plane of spirit. Or rather, it is hard to see that any activity can exist in stillness. The Quakers have an expression that exactly describes our natural attitude in spiritual things. They call it "creaturely activity," and they mean that the creature in us, that which the Bible calls the "natural man," is apt to push its activities outside of its own sphere of matter into the sphere of spirit, where it has no power, and where it can never accomplish anything. This is simply a law of its being. "The natural man receiveth not the things of the Spirit of God: for they are foolishness unto him; neither can he know them, because they are spiritually discerned."

The caterpillar, no matter how much it might try, could never fly, because on the caterpillar plane of life there is no flying power. But let this same caterpillar become a butterfly, and flying will be natural and easy. In the same way the "flesh" or the "natural man" cannot be active in spiritual things, because its sphere of life is not on the spiritual plane, but on the natural.

"So then they that are in the flesh cannot please God." This does not of course mean that man in the body cannot receive the things of God nor be subject to His law, but that the natural or fleshly man in us cannot, because it belongs to a different plane of life. And similarly the natural or fleshly activities in us cannot control spiritual forces, because they also belong to an entirely different plane.

> For though we walk in the flesh, we do not war after the flesh: (For the weapons of our warfare are not carnal, but mighty through God to the pulling down of strong holds;) Casting down imaginations, and every high thing that exalteth itself against the knowledge of God, and bringing into captivity every thought to the obedience of Christ (2 Corinthians 10:3–5).

No carnal, that is, fleshly, weapons can ever pull down spiritual strongholds, and no carnal activities can accomplish spiritual results. Therefore our strength in the region of spirit must necessarily be to "sit still" as to the activities of the creature, and to be alert only as to the activities of the Spirit.

> For thus saith the Lord God, the Holy One of Israel, In returning and rest shall ye be saved; in quietness and in confidence shall be your strength: and ye would not. But ye said, No; for we will flee upon horses; therefore shall ye flee: and, We will ride upon the swift; therefore shall they that pursue you be swift. One thousand shall flee at the rebuke of one; at the rebuke of five shall ye flee: till ye be left as a bea-

con upon the top of a mountain, and as an ensign on an hill (Isaiah 30:15–17).

The Israelites of old, like Christians now, could not believe that quietness and rest were the way of strength and deliverance; and they tried instead to "flee upon horses," and to "ride upon the swift," just as we now try to find our deliverance by earthly means and by creaturely activities. It is as useless for us as for them; and our defeats, as theirs were, are as a thousand to one. The truth is, the silent way is the only victorious way. A great student of Christian philosophy once said to me, "All things come to him who knows how to trust and be silent"; and the words are pregnant with meaning. A knowledge of this fact would immensely change our ways of working. Instead of the restless and wearying struggles of our present methods, we would "sit down" inwardly before the Lord, in "quietness and confidence," and would let the divine forces of His Spirit work out in silence the ends to which we aspire. You may not see or feel the operations of this silent force, but be assured it is always working mightily, and will work for you, if only you can get your spirit still enough to be carried along by the currents of its power.

> And Moses said unto the people, Fear ye not, stand still, and see the salvation of the Lord, which he will show to you to day: for the Egyptians whom ye have seen to day, ye shall see them again no more for ever (Exodus 14:13).

Only when we "stand still" can we see the salvation of the Lord. While full of bustle and hurry, we have no eyes to spare for God's work; our own work absorbs all our interest. Moreover, our creaturely activity, instead of helping, really hinders His working. Spiritual forces cannot have full flow when carnal forces usurp their place; and to see God's salvation fully worked out, we must let His power accomplish it all, and must not permit our own "carnal" working to interfere.

> Then said she, Sit still, my daughter, until thou know how the matter will fall: for the man will not be in rest, until he have finished the thing this day (Ruth 3:18).

To many this "sitting still" may seem like laziness, and they may naturally think that nothing can be accomplished under such conditions. But we are only to sit still because God works. Naomi could tell Ruth to sit still, because she had faith enough in Boaz to be able to add, "For the man will not be in rest until he have finished the matter this day." The Lord cannot rest while there remains anything unfinished for His people.

> For Zion's sake will I not hold my peace, and for Jerusalem's sake I will not rest, until the righteousness thereof go forth as brightness, and the salvation thereof as a lamp that burneth (Isaiah 62:1).

No mother can rest while her children are needing anything, and neither can God. Therefore, just as the child "sits still" in its little heart, in perfect confidence that the mother will care for it, so must we "sit still" in our hearts, in perfect confidence that our Father will care for us.

I say, sit still in our hearts, because this stillness of which I am writing is an inward stillness. It may also be an outward stillness as well, and I think the outward stillness often helps the inward. But, on the other hand, it may be accompanied with great outward activity; though never, I think, with bustle or hurry, for "he that believeth maketh not haste." But whether the body is active or still, the attitude of the spirit must always be one of stillness.

> And the work of righteousness shall be peace; and the effect of righteousness quietness and assurance for ever. And my people shall dwell in a peaceable habitation, and in sure dwellings, and in quiet resting places; When it shall hail, coming down on the forest; and the city shall be low in a low place (Isaiah 32:17–19).

There may be storms of hail outside; but within, the "habitation" of the spirit is a "quiet resting-place" in God. This sitting still, therefore, does not interfere with outward activity, but is, in fact, the source of its strength. If I am working at anything outwardly, and am inwardly at rest about it, I shall do it far more successfully than if I fret, and fume, and fuss inwardly. This is a matter of universal commonsense experience.

> Keep silence before me, O islands; and let the people renew their strength: let them come near; then let them speak: let us come near together to judgment (Isaiah 41:1).

Our strength is never renewed in noise and bustle. These only weaken and waste it. Try it for yourself, dear reader. The next time you find yourself in need of a renewal of strength, get still before the Lord. If possible, sit down in silence somewhere, and collect your restless and wandering spiritual faculties into a silence waiting upon Him, and see if strength does not flow into you from Him. This is what the old saints used to call "recollection"; and it was in this way they gained the wonderful spiritual vigor for which we so envy them.

> Be silent, O all flesh, before the Lord: for he is raised up out of his holy habitation (Zechariah 2:13).
> And he said, Go forth, and stand upon the mount before the Lord. And, behold, the Lord passed by, and a great and strong wind rent the mountains, and brake in pieces the rocks before the Lord; but the Lord was not in the wind: and after the wind an earthquake; but the Lord was not in the earthquake: And after the earthquake a fire; but the Lord was not in the fire: and after the fire a still small voice (1 Kings 19:11, 12).

Only in the "silence of all flesh" can the "still, small voice" be heard. A large part of the difficulty experienced by Christians in hearing the voice of the Lord arises, I am convinced, from the absence of this inward stillness. Our own internal clamor drowns His quiet speaking. We listen for His voice "in the wind" and "in the earthquake," expecting their thunder to sound above all our own clamoring; and because we are disappointed, we complain that He does not speak at all; when all the while, the "still small voice" of His love is waiting for the quiet in which it can be heard. I am convinced that there are many at this moment hungering for the voice of the Lord, who would hear it at once if they would but "be silent before Him" for a little while. This is the foundation thought of the silent meetings of the "Friends," even though it may be that their outward stillness does not always secure the perfect inward stillness that is the vital thing. All the saints of old have insisted upon stillness as a necessity of true communion with God, and have exhorted their followers to cultivate it; and every saint of the present day knows its value.

I remember a story of a little girl at her prayers, that impressed me very much. Her mother was in the next room, with the door ajar, and she heard the little trusting voice going through its childish petitions, and then adding quaintly, "And now, dear Jesus, I have said all I want to say to You, and I will listen to hear what You have to say to me." There came a few moments of perfect silence, and then a soft, satisfied, "Thank You, dear Jesus, that was very nice," and the little listener ran off to her play.

Try the baby's plan, dear grown-up Christian, and see if you, too, cannot get quiet enough inwardly to hear the "still small voice" of God.

> And David said to Solomon, My son, as for me, it was in my mind to build an house unto the name of the Lord my God: But the word of the Lord came to me, saying, Thou hast shed blood abundantly and hast made great wars: thou shalt not build an house unto my name, because thou hast shed much blood upon the earth in my sight. Behold, a son shall be born to thee, who shall be a man of rest; and I will give him rest from all his enemies round about: for his name shall be Solomon, and I will give peace and quietness unto Israel in his days. He shall build an house for my name; and he shall be my son, and I will be his father; and I will establish the throne of his kingdom over Israel for ever (1 Chronicles 22:7–9).

To know the indwelling of the Lord as a conscious experience, there must be inward quiet. Where there are wars and fightings inwardly, His presence cannot be realized. I do not mean that when the soul is in conflict the Lord has forsaken it. A thousand times, No! The Lord was with David just as truly as He was with Solomon; but it required a "man of rest" to build the house to His name, and not a man in the midst of wars. What I mean is only this, that His indwelling presence cannot be consciously realized when we are in the midst of internal wars; and that to have the conscious experience of His indwelling we must be at rest inwardly, and must know what it is to "keep silence" from all our fears and anxieties, and all our fussings and worryings.

> But the Lord is in his holy temple: let all the earth keep silence before him (Habakkuk 2:20).
> Whose adorning let it not be that outward adorning of plaiting the hair, and of wearing of gold, or of putting on of apparel; But let it be the hidden man of the heart, in that which is not corruptible, even the ornament of a meek and quiet spirit, which is in the sight of God of great price (1 Peter 3:3, 4).

Our active service may or may not be pleasing to the Lord, according to what is the motive behind it; but if we would cultivate something that can never fail to please Him, we will seek to have always that "meek and quiet spirit, which is in the sight of God of great price." Stop and think for a moment what an inestimable privilege it is to be able to offer to the Lord something that is of "great price" to Him, and see if we shall not be stirred up to cultivate more and more of this inward quietness of spirit, that knows no anxiety and no hurry.

> But we beseech you, brethren, that ye increase more and more; And that ye study to be quiet, and to do your own business, and to work with your own hands, as we commanded you (1 Thessalonians 4:10, 11).

"Study to be quiet," that is, study to dismiss all bustle and worry out of your inward life. Study also to "do your own business," and do not try to do the business of other people. A great deal of "creaturely activity" is expended in trying to do other people's business. It is often very hard to "sit still" when we see our friends, according to our ideas, mismanaging matters, and making such dreadful blunders. But the divine order, as it is also the best human order as well, is for each one of us to do our own business, and to refrain from meddling with the business of anyone else.

> Better is an handful with quietness, than both the hands full with travail and vexation of spirit (Ecclesiastes 4:6).
> Better is a dry morsel, and quietness therewith, than an house full of sacrifices with strife (Proverbs 17:1).

If this is true, and who can doubt it, in the earthly life, how much more true must it be in the spiritual life. There is nothing more distressing than the "travail and vexation of spirit," and the "house full of sacrifices with strife," that is so often the prevailing condition of the Christian heart. All of us know far too much of these sad conditions, and can speak from a bitter experience. We may feel that the Lord is feeding our souls with very "dry morsels," and may be tempted to make "sacrifices with strife" in order to procure for ourselves what seems to us more nourishing food. But if we have learned anything of the strength of stillness, we shall understand that far better is a "handful with quietness than both the hands full with travail and vexation of spirit," and shall be content with whatever morsels the Lord may give us, and rest in quiet peace until He shall give us more.

> But whoso hearkeneth unto me, shall dwell safely, and shall be quiet
> from fear of evil (Proverbs 1:33).

The key to this interior quietness of soul, is faith. To "hearken" to
the Lord does not simply mean to hear Him, but to hear Him in
faith, that is, to believe what He says.

> And to whom sware he that they should not enter into his rest, but to
> them that believed not? So we see that they could not enter in because
> of unbelief. Let us therefore fear, lest a promise being left us of entering
> into his rest, any of you should seem to come short of it. For unto us
> was the gospel preached, as well as unto them: but the word preached
> did not profit them, not being mixed with faith in them that heard it.
> For we which have believed do enter into rest (Hebrews 3:18, 19;
> 4:1–3).

In order to enter into this inward rest, our hearing must be "mixed
with faith"; that is, we must implicitly believe what the Lord has
said, and must never let in a question or a doubt as to the blessed
declarations He has made concerning His love and care for us. The
real fact is, that if we do believe these declarations, we cannot fail to
be at rest. No child can go on worrying or being frightened when
once it is convinced that its mother is at hand to protect it. Often it is
hard to convince the child of this, for its little heart is in too great a
flutter to hearken. But when once it really is convinced, all its trouble
vanishes. And just so will it be with us; "we which have believed do
enter into rest" always.

> But God, who is rich in mercy, for his great love wherewith he loved
> us, Even when we were dead in sins, hath quickened us together with
> Christ (by grace ye are saved;) And hath raised us up together, and
> made us sit together in heavenly places in Christ Jesus (Ephesians
> 2:4–6).

This is our rightful place, to be "seated" in heavenly places in
Christ Jesus, and to "sit still" there. But how few there are who make
it their actual experience! How few, indeed, think even that it is possible for them to "sit still" in these "heavenly places" in the everyday
life of a world so full of turmoil as this. We may believe perhaps that
to pay a little visit to these heavenly places on Sundays, or now and
then in times of spiritual exaltation, may be within the range of possibility; but to be actually "seated" there every day and all day long

is altogether another matter. And yet it is very plain that it is a universal command for Sundays and weekdays as well, and therefore, even in the life of the greatest turmoil, it must be possible.

I believe myself that this is the only way in which one can get through the weekdays of life with any sort of real success. A quiet spirit is of inestimable value in carrying on outward activities; and nothing so hinders the working of the hidden spiritual forces, upon which after all our success in anything really depends, as a spirit of unrest and anxiety.

To secure this inward stillness, but three things are necessary, and these are fully set forth in Lesson 4. (Yield, Trust, Obey.) When our affairs are really handed over to the Lord in absolute trust, and we are prepared to obey His will in regard to them all, there must be quiet of spirit. There is, in fact, no room or place for unrest.

> Be still, and know that I am God: I will be exalted among the heathen, I will be exalted in the earth. The Lord of hosts is with us; the God of Jacob is our refuge (Psalms 46:10, 11).

In order really to know God, this inward stillness is absolutely necessary. I remember when I first learned this. A time of great emergency had arisen in my life, when every part of my being seemed to throb with anxiety, and when the necessity for immediate and vigorous action seemed overpowering. And yet circumstances were such that I could do nothing, and the person who could, would not stir. For a little while it seemed as if I must fly to pieces with the inward turmoil, when suddenly the still small voice whispered in the depths of my soul, "Be still, and know that I am God." The word was with power, and I hearkened. I composed my body to perfect stillness, and I constrained my troubled spirit into quietness, and looked up and waited. And then I did "know" that it was God, God even in the very emergency, and in my very helplessness to meet it; and I rested in Him. He was exalted "among the heathen" and in my earth. It was an experience that I would not have missed for worlds. And I may add also, that out of this stillness seemed to arise a power to deal with the emergency that very soon brought it to a successful issue.

I learned then effectually the lesson that my "strength was to sit still."

I believe it is often helpful to compel the body to be still, as an aid to the quieting of the spirit; but where this cannot be, let me entreat all my readers to begin from this time onward to "sit still" in their hearts, sure that the Lord "will not be in rest until He have finished" the matter, whatever it may be, that concerns them.

Lesson 18

Wherefore Didst Thou Doubt?

FOUNDATION TEXT:—And immediately Jesus stretched forth his hand, and caught him, and said unto him, O thou of little faith, wherefore didst thou doubt?—Matthew 14:31.

"Wherefore didst thou doubt?" This is a most significant question. It is as though our Lord had said, "Knowing Me as thou dost, Peter, and having had experience of all My love and care for thee so long, how is it that thou canst doubt Me now? If I have called thee to come to Me on the water, of course I will enable thee to do so. What are boisterous winds or tossing waves to ME, who am the Creator and Ruler of them all? Wherefore dost thou doubt?"

This question is as full of significance now as it was on that stormy night in Galilee 1,800 years ago. Of thousands of Christians living on the earth at the present moment it might well be asked. For when winds are contrary and seas are stormy with us, doubts and fears are as near at hand to overwhelm us as they were near at hand to Peter; and the reproach, "O thou of little faith," applies as definitely to many of Christ's disciples now as it did to Peter then.

And there arose a great storm of wind, and the waves beat into the ship, so that it was now full. And he was in the hinder part of the ship, asleep on a pillow: and they awake him and say unto him, Master, carest thou not that we perish? And he arose, and rebuked the wind, and said unto the sea, Peace, be still. And the wind ceased, and there was a great calm. And he said unto them, Why are ye so fearful? how is it that ye have no faith? (Mark 4:37–40.)

171

The fright of these disciples was not caused by the great storm to which they were exposed, but by their own lack of faith. Storms cannot frighten people who are trusting in the Lord. Doubt is the foundation of every fear that can by any possibility assail the child of God.

"For whoso hearkeneth unto me, that is, whoso believes what I say, shall dwell safely, and shall be quiet from fear of evil." Most people, alas! do not hearken unto God, but they hearken instead to their own fears. The soul that really hearkens unto the Lord knows there is absolutely nothing to be afraid of, and will declare triumphantly with the Psalmist, "The Lord is my light and my salvation; whom shall I fear? the Lord is the strength of my life; of whom shall I be afraid?" And it will answer its own questions with the confident assertion, "Though an host should encamp against me, my heart shall not fear!" Not all the hosts of earth or hell can frighten the soul that "hearkens unto God."

Of course it will be understood that I am not in this lesson dealing with the doubts of unbelievers, such doubts as are called Agnostic doubts. It is the doubts of disciples I refer to, such doubts as Peter had, or those disciples in the little ship into which the waves were beating on that stormy evening long ago; doubts as to God's love for us and His care over us, doubts as to His wisdom, or as to His omnipotence, or as to His interest in our affairs, or as to His watchfulness, or as to His abiding presence with us. We all know the sort of doubts I mean, and have probably all been more or less plagued by them at one time or another in our lives.

> And thy life shall hang in doubt before thee; and thou shalt fear day and night, and shalt have none assurance of thy life. In the morning thou shalt say, Would God it were even! and at even thou shalt say, Would God it were morning! for the fear of thine heart wherewith thou shalt fear, and for the sight of thine eyes which thou shalt see (Deuteronomy 28:66, 67).

I believe there are many Christians whose experience could best be described in very much these same words. Their life (spiritual life) hangs in doubt before them continually, and they have no assurance of their life. Doubts eat into the very heart of everything. Nobody can have any comfort who indulges in doubts. A great many people have contracted such an inveterate habit of doubting, that no drunkard was ever more in bondage to his drink habit than they are to their doubt habit. And the worst of it is that they seem to have settled down under their doubts as to a sort of chronic malady, from which they suffer very much, but to which they must resign themselves as to a part of the necessary discipline of this earthly life. They even lament over their doubts as a man might lament over his rheumatism, and look upon their doleful experience as though it were an "interesting case" of especial and peculiar trial, which calls for the tenderest sympathy and the uttermost consideration! I appeal to my readers whether this is not a true description of a great deal of their religious life.

Now the vital question is, Wherefore do we doubt? Is doubt a necessary and integral part of the Christian religion; and if it is not, why has it gained such a foothold? To the first part of this question I would reply emphatically, that the whole testimony of Scripture, and the verdict of common sense as well, is utterly against doubting; and that as a truth doubting is always and everywhere, in the Bible and out of it, treated by God as a sin. We are, in fact, told plainly that the man who wavereth (*i.e.* doubteth) must not expect to receive anything of the Lord (James 1:6, 7). Faith, absolute and unconditional, is the universal requirement; and, in view of the character of the One whom we are called upon to trust, it is the only sensible and reasonable thing. It is amazing that we can be so idiotic as to doubt or question anything with which God, our unchangeable omnipotent God, has to do. Our Divine Master when on earth tried to convince us of the utter folly of doubt. One of His very last commands was this, "Let not your heart be troubled, neither let it be afraid"; and consequently when we indulge in doubts or fears, we are not only doing a very silly thing, but we are also directly disobeying Him. The grounds upon which He gives us this command is His own assurance that if there was any, even the slightest reason for fear, "He would have told us." Surely He would! We can trust His faithfulness and honesty this far, at least! Then, since He has not told us that there is any cause for fear or anxiety, but, on the contrary, has assured us that there is none, how is it that we can dare to doubt? I confess it is a mystery to me. As far as I can find out, Mohammedans do not doubt, neither do the worshipers of idols. It seems reserved for Christians to make a sort of religion of their doubting, and to look upon it as the indication of a humble and proper frame of mind. As if the doubting, which would be considered most unfilial and wicked in an earthly child towards its earthly father, becomes pious and beautiful in the child of God towards his Heavenly Father.

And yet I know well how reasonable and sensible our doubts seem. "Look, Peter," the tempter most probably said, "look at those roaring waves, and remember that such a thing was never heard of as that a man could walk on water. It is really presumptuous for you to try to do it. The Master does not mean for you actually to go to Him. It is only a figure of speech; and if you do not want to be drowned, you had better get back to a safe place on the ship as fast as you can." The amazing thing to me is, however, that Peter could listen for a moment to these suggestions of doubt, when he had heard the Master's command. And yet in the face of hundreds of similar commands and promises, Christians now listen to far worse suggestions of doubt, and even think they are pious and humble in so doing! It is simply amazing!

> If, then, God so clothe the grass, which is today in the field, and to morrow is cast into the oven; how much more will he clothe you, O ye of little faith? And seek not ye what ye shall eat, or what ye shall drink, neither be ye of doubtful mind. For all these things do the nations of the world seek after: and your Father knoweth that ye have need of these things (Luke 12:28–30).

To say that our Father "knoweth" we have a need, seemed to our Lord a sufficient guarantee that of course He would supply it. It is enough for the child if its mother knows that it has need of anything. Her mother-love compels her, if it lies within her power, to supply that need. And it is the same with God. He who made the mother's heart must have one at least equally as motherly; and to know we have a need, must mean that He will unfailingly supply it. If then we are of "doubtful mind," it is an implication on our part that either He does not know our need, or else that, knowing it, He does not care. Surely we cannot want to be guilty of such an insult towards God as this. Paul says, "I know whom I have believed, and therefore am persuaded that He is able to keep that which I have committed to Him." If we knew Him, as Paul did, we also should be equally persuaded; for we would see how utterly impossible it is that He could ever fail us. Men may fail us, but God never! Every doubt, therefore, is in reality a libel against God; for it is an implication that He who has promised is not faithful, but unfaithful, and that He cannot be fully trusted.

> Fear thou not; for I am with thee! be not dismayed; for I am thy God; I will strengthen thee; yea, I will help thee: yea, I will uphold thee with the right hand of my righteousness. . . . For I, the Lord thy God, will hold thy right hand, saying unto thee, Fear not; I will help thee. Fear not, thou worm Jacob, and ye men of Israel; I will help thee, saith the Lord, and thy redeemer, the Holy One of Israel (Isaiah 41:10, 13, 14).

The Bible is full of these "Fear nots," with their accompanying assurances that God will be with us, and will certainly care for us. If we believe these assurances, no enemies and no dangers, whether they are outward or inward, can cause us a moment's fear or doubt; for we will know that the Lord our God is stronger than any enemy the universe contains, and we will say with the Apostle, "If God be for me, who can be against me?"

> Yea, though I walk through the valley of the shadow of death, I will fear no evil: for thou art with me: thy rod and thy staff they comfort me (Psalms 23:4).

Not even the valley of the shadow of death can cause the trusting heart to fear. The fact of God's presence is enough always to make the "fearful heart" strong, let the circumstances be what they may.

> Strengthen ye the weak hands, and confirm the feeble knees. Say to them that are of a fearful heart, Be strong, fear not; behold your God will come with vengeance, even God with a recompense: he will come and save you (Isaiah 35:3, 4).
>
> For God hath not given us the spirit of fear; but of power, and of love, and of a sound mind (2 Timothy 1:7).

The "spirit of fear" does not belong to the Christian religion. It is never enumerated among the "fruits of the Spirit." It is not given to us from God. On the contrary, it is always condemned as being alien to the whole idea of Christianity, and as coming purely and only from unbelief.

> Yea, they spake against God; they said, Can God furnish a table in the wilderness? Behold, he smote the rock, that the waters gushed out, and the streams overflowed; can he give bread also? can he provide flesh for his people? Therefore the Lord heard this, and was wroth: so a

fire was kindled against Jacob, and anger also came up against Israel;
Because they believed not in God, and trusted not in his salvation
(Psalms 78:19–22).

All doubts are a "speaking against God." I know a great many of
my readers will start at this and exclaim, "Oh, no, that is a mistake.
Doubts often arise from humility. We feel ourselves to be so unworthy of the love and care of God that we cannot believe it is possible
for Him to love or care for us. It is not that we doubt Him, but we
doubt ourselves." This sounds very plausible; but let us see what it
amounts to. Does God's love for us depend on the kind of people we
are? Does He love only good people? or does He love sinners? The
Bible says, "God commendeth His love toward us in that while we
were yet sinners Christ died for us." And again it says: "But God
who is rich in mercy, for His great love wherewith He loved us, even
when we were dead in sins, hath quickened us together with Christ."
Can it be called humility to question this, and to doubt whether,
after all, He really does love us who are sinners? We would not think
it humility on the part of our children, if, when they were naughty,
they should begin to doubt our love for them, and, because they had
been disobedient, should be anxious lest we should neglect them and
fail to protect their interests. True humility, no matter how unworthy
it may feel itself to be, instead of creating doubts, extinguishes them,
because it would not presume to doubt God's promises of love and
care.

"We love Him because He first loved us," is what the Bible says.
But we are continually tempted to reverse this order and say, "He
loves us because we first loved Him"; and then, finding our own love
so weak and poor, we naturally begin to doubt whether He loves us
at all. We can never do anything but doubt, just so long as we think
God's love for us is dependent upon the amount of our love for Him.
But to think this, is to fly in the face of every word He has said about
it. Our duty, therefore, is to throw aside every doubt, and to let ourselves go in an unwavering belief in the unmerited but unfailing love
of God.

But ye, beloved, building up yourselves on your most holy faith,
praying in the Holy Ghost, Keep yourselves in the love of God, looking
for the mercy of our Lord Jesus Christ unto eternal life (Jude 20, 21).

To keep ourselves in the love of God, or, in other words, to keep ourselves in God's love, does not mean, as so many think, to keep ourselves loving Him. It means to settle ourselves down, as it were, into His love as an absolute and unalterable fact, to take up our abode in it, and to stay in it forever. It means never to doubt His love, never to question it, never to fear losing it; but to believe in it, and trust it, despite all seemings to the contrary, utterly and steadfastly and for ever.

> For this cause I bow my knees unto the Father of our Lord Jesus Christ, Of whom the whole family in heaven and earth is named, That he would grant you, according to the riches of his glory, to be strengthened with might by his Spirit in the inner man; That Christ may dwell in your hearts by faith; that ye, being rooted and grounded in love, may be able to comprehend with all saints what is the breadth, and length, and depth, and height; And to know the love of Christ, which passeth knowledge, that ye might be filled with all the fulness of God (Ephesians 3:14–19).

The soul that is "rooted and grounded" in the love of God, and that keeps itself there unwaveringly, has got into a region where doubt is impossible. For who could doubt love? It is in the very nature of love to do the very best it possibly can for those it loves. This is its law. Therefore, when once we believe in the love of God, we know, without a shadow of doubt, that we cannot possibly have anything to fear.

> There is no fear in love; but perfect love casteth out fear: because fear hath torment. He that feareth is not made perfect in love (1 John 4:18).

He that feareth has never yet fully believed in the "huge tenderness" of the love of God!

> Pining souls, come nearer Jesus,
> And, oh, come not doubting thus,
> But with love that trusts more bravely
> His huge tenderness for us.

Doubts are a complete barrier to any success in the Christian life. Spiritual things work altogether by the law of faith, and doubts are barriers that effectually hinder the working of this law.

> He that overcometh shall inherit all things; and I will be his God, and he shall be my son. But the fearful, and unbelieving, and the abominable, and murderers, and whoremongers, and sorcerers, and idolaters, and all liars, shall have their part in the lake which burneth with fire and brimstone, which is the second death (Revelation 21:7, 8).

It is a most significant fact that among the sins which are here declared to plunge a soul into the "lake of fire" that of being "fearful and unbelieving" heads the list. All that this means I do not know, but I am certain it must mean this much, that to be fearful and unbelieving is as absolute a hindrance to the spiritual life as many things which we consider far greater sins. And this leaves us no alternative as to whether or not we shall go on indulging in the habit of doubt. We dare not do it. We must get rid of our doubts somehow. The only question is, How? To this I would reply that there is only one way. We must GIVE THEM UP. We must make a surrender of them to the Lord, and must trust Him to deliver us from their power. Doubts are a "speaking against God," and are consequently sin. They are not an infliction, but a rebellion. We can never indulge in them for a single moment without disobeying the Lord, who has left us, as His last command, this law, "Let not your heart be troubled, neither let it be afraid." No matter how plausible our doubts may seem, we simply MUST turn our backs on them, and refuse to entertain them for a moment. I believe myself it is a good thing to sign a pledge against doubting, just as one signs a pledge against drink. This means that you give up all liberty to doubt, that, in short, you make an entire consecration or surrender of your doubting. And if you do this, the Lord, as He always does when anything is surrendered to Him, will take possession of your doubts, and will deliver you from their power.

You must hand your doubting over to Him, as you do your temper or your pride, and must trust Him to deliver you from doubting, just as you do to deliver you from getting angry. The great point is to give up the liberty to doubt. The trouble lies in the fact that, in this matter of doubting, most people reserve to themselves a little liberty, because they feel it is impossible always to trust and never to doubt. "I do not want to doubt anymore," we will say, or "I hope I shall not"; but it is hard to come to the point of saying, "I will not. I give up all liberty to doubt forever." But no surrender is really effectual until it reaches the point of saying "I will not." Therefore our only hope for victory lies in an utter surrender of all liberty to doubt forever.

I do not mean that doubts will not come. As long as we are in this body of flesh I suppose we shall be subject to the temptation to doubt. But while we cannot help the temptation coming, we can help entertaining it, and giving it an abiding place in our hearts. We must treat every temptation to doubt as a temptation to sin, and must refuse to entertain it for a single moment. It will help us in this if we begin to assert by faith the exact opposite of our doubt. Doubts always fly when faith appears on the scene. If the doubt, for instance, says, "God does not love you," faith must declare more emphatically than ever, "God does love me. He says He does, and I know it is true." Kill your doubts by refusing to listen to them for a moment. Doubts cannot live where they find no nourishment.

Therefore, dear doubting souls, this is what you must do. You must hand over your doubting to the Lord and must "set your faces like a flint" never to indulge in doubts again.

> For the Lord God will help me; therefore shall I not be confounded; therefore have I set my face like a flint, and I know that I shall not be ashamed (Isaiah 50:7).

A little experience in the life of one of my children may be helpful. One night as I was tucking her up in bed she said to me, "Well, Mother, I have had my first doubt." "What was it?" I asked in great surprise. "Oh," she replied, "Satan told me that God did not love me, because I was such a naughty little girl; and he said I was a foolish child to believe God loved me, even if my mother did say He did." "What did you say?" I asked. "Oh," she replied, "I just said, 'Satan, I am going to believe it, and I WILL believe it; so there!' And then he did not bother me anymore."

Of course I was delighted at the child's sensible way of dealing with her doubts, and encouraged her all I could always to treat them after this fashion; and did not suppose I should hear of them again. But the next night after she was in bed, and I went for my goodnight kiss, she greeted me with the words, "Well, Mother, Satan has been at it again." "What did he say this time?" I asked. "Why, he said," she replied, "that the Bible was not true, and that only foolish people believed it." "And what did you answer him?" I asked. "Oh," she replied, "I just said, 'Satan, shut your mouth!' and he ran away as fast as he could."

That little child had learned how to treat her doubts. May the blessed Spirit teach each one of us how to do the same!

A TALK WITH ST. PETER

O Peter, wherefore didst thou doubt?
In truth the scud flew fast about;
But He was there, whose walking foot
Could make the wandering hills take root;

And He had said, "Come down to Me,"
Else had thy foot not touched the sea;
Christ did not call thee to thy grave;
Was it the *boat* that made thee brave?

Easy for *thee*, who wast not there,
To think thou, more than I, could'st dare!
It hardly fits thee though to mock,
Scared as thou wast that railway shock!
Who said'st this morn, "Wife, we must go;
The plague will soon be here, I know."
Who, when thy child slept (not to death),
Said'st, "Nothing now is worth a breath!"

True! True! Great Fisherman! I stand
Rebuked by waves seen from the land!
Even the lashing of the spray,
The buzzing fears of any day,
Rouse anxious doubt lest I should find
God neither in the spray nor wind.
But now and then, as once to thee,
The Master turns and looks at me!

And now to Him I turn. My Lord,
Help me to fear nor fire nor sword;
Let not the cross itself appal!
Know I not Thee, the Lord of all!

Let reeling brain nor fainting heart
Wipe out the sureness that Thou art!
Oh, deeper, Thou, than doubt can go,
Make my poor hope cry out, "I know!"

And so when Thou shalt please to say,
"Come to My side," some stormy way,
My feet, attuning to Thy will,
Shall, heaved and tossed, walk toward Thee still.
No leaden heart shall sink me where
Prudence is crowned with cold despair;
But I shall reach and clasp Thy hand,
And, on the sea, forget the land!

                                        GEORGE MAC DONALD

Lesson 19

Temptation

FOUNDATION TEXT:—Blessed is the man that endureth temptation: for when he is tried, he shall receive the crown of life, which the Lord hath promised to them that love him.— James 1:12.

If there is one thing more than another that we need to have on a good sound commonsense basis, it is the subject of temptation; for nothing, I feel convinced, is more misunderstood. Moreover, temptation is an affair of every day, and in a book of lessons for everyday life, it is of vital importance.

The first commonsense thing that I would say concerning temptation is, that temptation is not sin. The second thing I would say is the same, and the third thing is the same also. It may seem to some as if this hardly needed to be said so emphatically, because everyone must already know it; but I believe, on the contrary, that very few really know it. People often assent to a thing as a theory, which practically they do not in the least believe; and this is just one of these things. No doubt everyone who reads this lesson will say he entirely unites with my proposition that temptation is not sin; but, as a matter of practical experience, how many act on this belief? Our foundation text tells us that it is a blessed thing to endure temptation; but do we really believe it to be a blessed thing? Do we not mostly feel, instead, that it is a cursed thing; and that we must be dreadful sinners just because we are tempted? A flood of evil thoughts is poured into our souls, proud thoughts, unkind thoughts, malicious thoughts, jealous thoughts. They are thoughts we loathe, and yet that we seem to originate; and we feel that we must be very wicked and very far off from

182

God to be able to have such thoughts at all. It is as though a burglar should break into a man's house to steal, and when the master of the house tries to resist him and drive him out, should turn around and accuse the owner of being himself the thief! It is the enemy's grand ruse for entrapping us. He whispers his suggestions of evil into our hearts, and then turns around and says, "Oh, how wicked you must be to think of such things! It is very plain you cannot be a child of God; for if you were, it would have been impossible for such dreadful thoughts to have entered your heart." This reasoning sounds so very plausible, that the Christian feels as if it must be true, and is plunged into the depths of discouragement and despair. But the divine teaching about temptation and the teaching of common sense as well, is very different.

> My brethren, count it all joy when ye fall into divers temptations; Knowing this, that the trying of your faith worketh patience. But let patience have her perfect work, that ye may be perfect and entire, wanting nothing (James 1:2–4).

If it is a sin to be tempted, should we be exhorted to "count it all joy" when we are tempted? Is it not rather a plain indication that temptation is one of God's divine instruments in our life discipline, and that without it we could never become "perfect and entire, wanting nothing"?

> Wherein ye greatly rejoice, though now for a season, if need be, ye are in heaviness through manifold temptations: That the trial of your faith, being much more precious than of gold that perisheth, though it be tried with fire, might be found unto praise and honour and glory at the appearing of Jesus Christ (1 Peter 1:6, 7).

Temptations try our faith; and we are worth nothing if we are not tried. They develop our spiritual virtues; and this development is essential to our true growth. How shallow would be our spirituality if it were not for the discipline of temptation! There is, therefore, in the divine plan evidently a "needs be" for the manifold temptations that beset us on every hand during the "season" of this earthly life. The "trial of our faith" is so much more precious to the Lord, and so much more valuable for us, than any present comfort or ease, that, much as He loves us, and, indeed, because He loves us, He is willing even to see us "in heaviness," on account of our temptations. This was His way with the children of Israel. When God took them into the promised land, He did not drive out at once all their enemies, but left some to "prove them," that He might know whether or not they would "hearken unto the commandments of the Lord." (*See* Judges 2:21–23; 3:1–4.)

I have sometimes thought that temptation is to our soul's health what vaccination is to our body's health, a process by which we are prepared for the victory over far worse attacks of far worse diseases.

> For thou, O God, hast proved us: thou hast tried us, as silver is tried. Thou broughtest us into the net; thou laidst affliction upon our loins. Thou hast caused men to ride over our heads; we went through fire and through water: but thou broughtest us out into a wealthy place (Psalms 66:10–13).

Silver is tried that it may be purified, and we are tried that we may be at last "brought out into a wealthy place."

Even of our Lord it is said that He "learned obedience by the things that He suffered"; and among the worst of these things must have been His temptations.

> For we have not an high priest which cannot be touched with the feeling of our infirmities; but was in all points tempted like as we are, yet without sin. Let us therefore come boldly unto the throne of grace, that we may obtain mercy, and find grace to help in time of need (Hebrews 4:15, 16).
>
> For in that he himself hath suffered being tempted, he is able to succour them that are tempted (Hebrews 2:18).

If we believe that our Lord was really tempted "in all points" like as we are, we cannot but be convinced that temptation is not sin, and that it is possible to have temptations of every kind, and yet be "without sin." We may be sure of this, also, that wherever temptation is, there is the Lord, waiting to succour. "Where wert thou, Lord, while I was being tempted?" cried the saint in the desert. "Close beside thee all the while, my son, giving thee the needed grace to conquer thy temptation," was the tender reply.

> There hath no temptation taken you but such as is common to man: but God is faithful, who will not suffer you to be tempted above that ye are able; but will with the temptation also make a way to escape, that ye may be able to bear it (1 Corinthians 10:13).

Fénelon says concerning temptation: "We must never be astonished at temptations, be they never so outrageous. On this earth all is temptation. Crosses tempt us by irritating our pride, and prosperity by flattering it. Our life is a continual combat, but one in which Jesus Christ fights for us. While temptations rage around us, we must pass on unmoved, as the traveler overtaken by a storm simply wraps his cloak more closely about him, and pushes on more vigorously towards his destined home."

The Lord knoweth how to deliver the godly out of temptations . . . (2 Peter 2:9).

Since the Lord "knoweth how" to deliver us out of temptation, He is surely the One to whom we should apply for deliverance; for it is very plain that we do not "know how" to deliver ourselves. There is not one of us who has not had practical proof of our own inability to deliver ourselves, so that I do not need to argue on this point. And yet, so foolish are we and ignorant, that most of us go on trying in the same old ineffectual ways, vainly thinking that if we only try harder, we shall certainly succeed at last. Our usual plan is to scold ourselves, and exhort ourselves, and weep over ourselves, and suffer agonies of remorse, and repent in dust and ashes; and then make stronger and more binding resolutions than ever, and try again, only to be again defeated.

Sometimes, it is true, we seem to conquer for a little while, and we rejoice over our victory, and think it will be permanent; when suddenly all our defenses seem to be taken from us, and we are overcome worse than ever. We wonder why this is, and often cannot help feeling that in some way we have been hardly treated by God, that, after all our efforts, such failures should be allowed to come. But the truth is, that there is only one "way of escape" from the power of temptation; and because we have not taken that "way" our failure is inevitable. We may resist this fact as much as we please, and may try every other possible plan, but sooner or later we have got to come back to the simple truth that there is only one Deliverer from temptation, and that that Deliverer is the Lord; and only one way of victory, and that that way is by faith.

When thou goest out to battle against thine enemies, and seest horses and chariots, and a people more than thou, be not afraid of them: for the Lord thy God is with thee, which brought thee up out of the land of Egypt. And it shall be, when ye are come nigh unto the battle, that the priest shall approach and speak unto the people, And shall say unto them, Hear, O Israel, ye approach this day unto battle against your enemies: let not your hearts faint; fear not, and do not tremble, neither be ye terrified because of them; For the Lord your God is he that goeth with you, to fight for you against your enemies, to save you (Deuteronomy 20:1–4).

"The Lord your God is He that goeth with you to fight for you against your enemies, to save you." This is the whole secret. I once asked a Christian, whose life of victory over temptation had greatly impressed me, what was his secret. He replied that it all lay in this, that the Lord fought for him and he held his peace. "Once," he said, "I used to feel that I had to do the fighting myself; and it always seemed to me that the Lord was behind me to help me if the emergency became too great, but that for the most part He looked on, and left the fighting to me. But now," he continued, "I put the Lord in front, and He does the fighting, while I look on and behold the victory."

In Ephesians we have a description of what the Christian's armor is; and this will further elucidate the subject.

Wherefore take unto you the whole armour of God, that ye may be able to withstand in the evil day, and having done all, to stand. Stand therefore, having your loins girt about with truth, and having on the breastplate of righteousness; And your feet shod with the preparation of the gospel of peace; Above all, taking the shield of faith, wherewith ye shall be able to quench all the fiery darts of the wicked. And take the helmet of salvation, and the sword of the Spirit, which is the word of God: Praying always with all prayer and supplication in the Spirit, and watching thereunto with all perseverance and supplication for all saints (Ephesians 6:13–18).

"Loins girt with truth," the "breastplate of righteousness," the "shield of faith," the "helmet of salvation," and the "sword of the Spirit, which is the word of God,"—all this is the armor of faith. Our Lord used this armor in His conflict with temptation in the wilderness. (*See* Luke 4:1–13.) This story, it seems to me, gives us a very vivid insight into the reality of the declaration that He was "in all points" tempted like as we are; and it also shows us how we are to conquer. The weapon He used was the "sword of the Spirit," which is, the Apostle tells us, the "word of God." He met each temptation with some saying out of the Bible, introducing them all by the words "It is written." I believe that the truth as it is revealed in the Scriptures of truth, is always our most effectual weapon against temptation. I say weapon, because I do not mean that it is our power. The power to conquer is from the Lord alone, but the weapons are put into our hands; and, to my mind, chief among these is the one used by Christ, that is, the word or truth of God. Practically I believe that there is nearly always some "It is written" with which we can meet and conquer almost every form of temptation.

I remember an occasion in my own life when I proved this. I had just laid down a new carpet in my living room, and was very desirous of keeping it fresh. My husband wanted to have a Bible class of rough working men with their hobnailed shoes to meet there every week, but I objected greatly, and felt very sure my nice new carpet would be entirely spoiled. But I found I was not comfortable, as a Christian woman, in placing myself in the position of putting the claims of a carpet above the claims of human souls, and I was sorely tossed and troubled. Then I bethought me of this sword of the Spirit, and wondered if I could use it in this case, thinking to myself that there could not surely be any "it is written" about carpets. However I took up my sword and began to say inwardly and rather forlornly "It is written," when there flashed into my mind—Yes, it *is* written, "take joyfully the spoiling of your goods." I confronted the enemy with this "sword of the Spirit," and it conquered for me. I was henceforward content to have my carpet or anything else, if necessary, "spoiled" in the service of the Lord.

I know by a thousand experiences that in every conflict with the temptation to doubt the love and care of God, there is no weapon so effectual as this sword of the Spirit. All doubts must necessarily fly before the confident assertion of some one or more of the innumerable assertions in the Bible of the all-embracing, unchangeable love of God. I have often routed a whole army of doubts by the simple words, repeated in unwavering faith, "It is written, that God is love!" Try it, dear reader, and see.

> Ye are they which have continued with me in my temptations. And I appoint unto you a kingdom, as my Father hath appointed unto me; That ye may eat and drink at my table in my kingdom, and sit on thrones judging the twelve tribes of Israel (Luke 22:28–30).

One great mistake we make about temptations is to feel as if the time spent in enduring them was all lost time. Days pass, perhaps, and we have been so beset with temptations as to feel as if we had made no progress. But it often happens that we have been serving the Lord far more truly while thus "continuing with Him" in temptation, than we could have done in our times of comparative freedom from it. Temptation is as much an attack against God as against ourselves, and we are fighting His battles quite as much as our own when we resist it. Moreover the "kingdom" which has been "appointed" to us can only come through this pathway of manifold temptations. The Apostle, when enumerating the qualifications and characteristics of those who had entered this kingdom, and had been patterns of faith in past ages, names temptation as one of the chief.

> They were stoned, they were sawn asunder, were tempted, were slain with the sword: they wandered about in sheepskins and goatskins: being destitute, afflicted, tormented; (Of whom the world was not worthy) (Hebrews 11:37, 38).

When next we are tempted, let us remember that those "of whom the world was not worthy" were tempted also, and we shall not be so discouraged. Discouragement is the very worst thing possible with which to meet temptation. If we are afraid of falling, we are almost sure to fall. A very wise writer on Christian experience once said that in order to overcome temptation a cheerful confidence that we shall overcome is the first thing, and the second thing, and the third thing, and the thing all the way through. The power of temptation lies largely in the fainting of our own hearts. The children of Israel were continually warned against this. No matter how terrible their enemies might seem, God's word always was, "Dread not, neither be afraid of them." And the reason given was invariably the same, "The Lord shall fight for you, and ye shall hold your peace." (*See* Exodus 14:13, 14; Deuteronomy 1:20–30.)

The Lord fights for us now just as really as He fought for the Israelites then; and we have no more business to be discouraged at our enemies than they had. We all see clearly that it was no sin for them to have enemies to fight, and we ought to see as clearly that it is no sin for us. Temptation, therefore, is under no circumstances to be regarded as a sin.

Sometimes, however, our discouragement arises from what we think is a righteous grief and disgust at ourselves, that such things can be any temptation to us. It seems as if we must be great sinners, or we could not be so tempted. But if we probe it to the bottom, we shall find that this feeling really arises from a mortified self-love. We have expected better things of ourselves than to be open to the possibility of such temptations, and we are sorely disappointed in ourselves; and are discouraged in consequence. This mortification and discouragement over our temptations are really a far worse condition than the temptations themselves, for they arise altogether from wounded vanity and self-love. Discouragement is never a fruit of humility, but always of pride.

> But every man is tempted, when he is drawn away of his own lust, and enticed. Then when lust hath conceived, it bringeth forth sin; and sin, when it is finished, bringeth forth death (James 1:14, 15).

It is no sin to be "enticed"; the sin comes only when we yield to the enticement. The word translated "lust" here is the same word that is used by our Lord when He said in Luke 22:15, "With desire have I desired to eat this Passover with you." It signifies a great wish for something. Now it is no sin to desire anything. I may see an orange in a shop window, and feel a desire for it, but this is not a sin. It is only when the desire "conceives" or begets theft, that sin enters. A great many tenderhearted Christians torture themselves with anxious self-examinations to see whether they may not have yielded at least a sort of half-consent in the moment of temptation. Fénelon says this is all wrong. He tells us that by examining too closely whether we have not been guilty of some unfaithfulness, we incur the risk of being again entangled in the temptation, after we have repulsed it. We ought to treat ourselves in such matters with as much care as we would treat our watches. If we fancy a watch is out of order, we are never so foolish as to take it apart and examine it ourselves in order to discover what is wrong. We are too well aware of the delicate nature of a watch's inside machinery to risk meddling with it. But we take it to a jeweler, who, having made watches, understands them, and can discover without risk what is the matter with them; and who, above all, knows how to put them in order again. And similarly, only the God, who made the delicate machinery of our inward being, is able to examine it without risk, or can know how to put it in order. The only safe thing to do, therefore, in the matter of temptation is simply, and without self-analysis, to commit ourselves to the Lord, and leave with Him the management of the whole matter.

> Be sober, be vigilant; because your adversary the devil, as a roaring lion, walketh about, seeking whom he may devour: Whom resist stedfast in the faith (1 Peter 5:8, 9).

It is no sin to hear the "roarings" of the devil, but it becomes sin if we stop and "roar" with him, or yield to his roarings. It is no sin to hear wicked men swearing along the street: it only becomes sin when we stop and join in with them. An old writer says, "Eye not the temptation, but eye the Lord"; and this expresses a profound truth. I believe it is often unwise even to pray much about our temptations, for the fact of praying keeps our mind fixed on them. The best way is a simple turning of the heart to the Lord, as a child to its mother, looking away from the temptation, and "looking unto Jesus," and leaving Him to deal with it as He pleases.

Fénelon says concerning this: "A direct struggle with temptations only serves to augment them. We should simply turn away from the evil, and draw nearer to God. A little child on perceiving a monster, does not wait to fight with it, and will scarcely turn its eyes toward it, but quickly shrinks into the bosom of its mother, sure of safety there. If we do otherwise, and in our weakness attempt to attack our enemies, we shall find ourselves wounded, if not totally defeated; but by remaining in the simple presence of God, we shall find instant supplies of strength for our support."

> Have not I commanded thee? Be strong and of a good courage; be not afraid, neither be thou dismayed: for the Lord thy God is with thee whithersoever thou goest (Joshua 1:9).
>
> For whatsoever is born of God overcometh the world: and this is the victory that overcometh the world, even our faith. Who is he that over-

cometh the world, but he that believeth that Jesus is the Son of God? (1 John 5:4, 5).

It is God's purpose that we who are born of Him should overcome the world; but we can only overcome in one way, and that is, not by struggle, or effort, or conflict, but by faith. We must put the Lord between ourselves and our temptations. We must meet them with a confident trust in His power and willingness to conquer them for us, and must be sure of victory beforehand. And above all, we must not blame ourselves for being tempted, but must remember always that "blessed is the man who endureth temptation," and must obey the the command to "count it all joy when we fall into divers temptations."

"Be of good cheer," says our Divine Master, "for I have overcome the world." It is an immense help in meeting temptation to meet it as an already conquered foe. In earthly battles, the defeated army is disorganized and surrenders, the moment they find out that the opposite side has discovered their defeat. In our Civil War in America the war was prolonged far beyond the necessary time, because the North had not yet found out that the South was defeated; and the South knew this, and kept up the fight. But the moment the South found that the North had discovered the fact of their defeat, they collapsed without another battle. Sin is for us an already conquered foe. The Lord Jesus Christ has met and conquered it, and we are, if we only knew it, more than conquerors in Him. Like Jehoshaphat and the children of Israel, if we will go out to battle against our enemies singing songs of victory, the Lord will set ambushments against them, and when we reach them, behold, they will all be "dead bodies." (*See* 2 Chronicles 20:1–30.)

> Then they returned, every man of Judah and Jersualem, and Jehoshaphat in the forefront of them, to go again to Jerusalem with joy; for the Lord had made them to rejoice over their enemies. And they came to Jerusalem with psalteries and harps and trumpets unto the house of the Lord. And the fear of God was on all the kingdoms of those countries, when they had heard that the Lord fought against the enemies of Israel. So the realm of Jehoshaphat was quiet: for his God gave him rest round about (2 Chronicles 20:27–30).

"So the realm of Jehoshaphat was quiet: for his God gave him rest round about." These lessons are closed with an earnest prayer that they may be used of the Lord to help some souls into this same "realm of quiet" in their everyday lives; to the end that they, too, as was Israel, may be a testimony to all who know them, of the reality of a God who always gives to those who trust in Him, "rest round about."